CODE
PEND
ENCE

Codependence
FIRST EDITION

Copyright © 2019 Amy Long
All rights reserved
Printed in the United States of America

ISBN 978·1·880834·12·1
DESIGN ≈ SEVY PEREZ
Adobe Caslon Pro, Brandon Grotesque, & ITC Caslon 224

This book is published by the

Cleveland State University Poetry Center
csupoetrycenter.com
2121 Euclid Avenue, Cleveland, Ohio 44115-2214

and is distributed by

SPD / Small Press Distribution, Inc.
spdbooks.org
1341 Seventh Street Berkeley, California 94710-1409

A CATALOG RECORD FOR THIS TITLE IS
AVAILABLE FROM THE LIBRARY OF CONGRESS

THIS IS A WORK OF NONFICTION

To protect the privacy of healthcare providers and other individuals who appear in
the book, some names have been changed. Where necessary, details related to specific
locations or businesses have also been altered. No characters, places, or events have been
composited or conflated. Everything here is true to the best of my recollection,
but memory and its interpretation are fallible.

All events depicted occurred before April 2016,
when major changes to opioid-prescribing praxes took effect.

CODEPENDENCE

AMY LONG

RELAPSE

1. I tell my mother that I've started taking opioids again. "Not the way I took them last time," I say. When I say *last time*, I mean the time she knows about. The time when I wasn't eighteen and nineteen. The time when I wasn't taking them for fun. When I say *last time*, I mean the five years during which I buried my headaches under fistfuls of round blue oxycodone pills, 300 milligrams every day. "It won't be like last time," I promise when she starts crying and I start crying and for a minute I think she really means it when she says, "You can do what you want, but you're on your own. I can't go through that again." When she says *that again*, she means the way I scurried around New York scavenging pharmacies for the kind and number of pills I needed; she's talking about the death rattle in my voice when I couldn't find them. When she says *that again*, she means the eight months I spent on Suboxone and the four weeks I spent detoxing in the bed where she doesn't sleep anymore, in the house where she no longer lives.

2. When her mother died, my mother stayed in bed for nine years. She lay on top of the covers and stared at the TV without really watching it. She wore loose-fitting house dresses designed for tourists, printed with white fish that swam in straight lines down to her knees. Sometimes she ran errands in them. She'd make dinner around sunset but then sit down at the kitchen table and watch my sisters and me eat the pot roast or lemon chicken she rarely

touched. When our dad took his plate to the computer and ate in front of his online cribbage match, she moved to the couch and watched CNN until she fell asleep. In the mornings, she hovered by the front door as my sisters and I pulled on our backpacks and headed out to the Jeep we shared. We were sixteen. "Cher says I've been depressed for a long time," my mom told me; I was 25, and she and our father had recently divorced. She'd started seeing a therapist. "I thought you'd been depressed since Memaw died," I said. She paused. "You knew that?"

3. My sisters and I are triplets. Beth went to med school in Alabama, did her residency in California and a fellowship at the most prestigious hospital in the country. Chelsea practices law in our hometown; her office is in the same complex as our dad's insurance agency and a few miles from our mom's new house. We don't call our parents "our mom" or "my dad." We say "the mom" and "the dad." Chelsea eats lunch with the dad every day, but I can't tell whether she or Beth is his favorite. I only know that I am not. When I visit Destin, we'll go out to eat and run into one of the dad's friends. "Is this the doctor or the lawyer?" the friend will ask. "I'm the other one," I say, and I'm joking, but the dad grimaces like he knows I'm right while I explain that I'm working on a graduate degree in creative writing. After I finished my first master's, in women's studies, I got a job with the ACLU in California. The dad worked himself into a rage that could have launched his career as a Fox News host. He said I was a communist and he was a capitalist and that my working for the ACLU was like taking his head and rubbing it in sand. The dad loves me, but I'm not sure he likes me. Not the way he likes Beth and Chelsea. The mom used to tell me that wasn't true. "Of course your father likes you," she'd say. Now she tells me not to worry about it. "He doesn't understand people who aren't like him."

4. I'd called the mom earlier that day, but I hadn't mentioned opioids. I don't call her as much as I used to; it feels like lying, talking to her on pills I haven't told her about. If she doesn't know I'm taking opioids again, she won't understand why I need them. She won't know when I tell her I wrote for six hours today that, without the opioids, I might have gotten in 45 minutes of chain smoking and deleting sentences. She'll think I'm able to work through my headaches or that they've gotten better even though I can't and they haven't. If I call her on one of the days when I won't let myself take any pills, I'll have to explain that I don't really feel like talking, and she'll wonder why I did feel like talking the day before. She asks me whether the lidocaine my pain doctor's wife injects into myofascial trigger points relieves my headaches. I can't say that it does, but neither can I say, "The Opana he prescribed sure helps, though."

5. The mom came with me to my first appointment at the Blacksburg Center for Pain Management. I would start my second year in Virginia Tech's MFA program in a few weeks. She thought the lidocaine treatments sounded promising. I thought the Christian paraphernalia around the office made her more comfortable, convinced her I'd found a good doctor who wouldn't write me opioids. The second time, I went alone. I knew I would leave with a painkiller prescription. I'd planned it all out. I just had to cry a little after Lisa injected me and wonder aloud whether I could endure this pain while I waited for the lidocaine to work, if it did at all. She said her husband had a cancellation and would talk to me if I could wait. I waited. Dr. Piven offered me oxycodone, Dilaudid, or Opana. I pretended I'd never heard of Opana and let him explain oxymorphone to me. "Whatever you think is best," I said and walked out with a prescription for a drug that my junkie ex-boyfriend once described as better than heroin. But when I got home and took one, I only felt the high in my body; I hadn't really taken opioids in a year, and I felt like I should have gotten

more out of something that strong. I had to crush the pills and snort them to get any headache relief at all.

6. The mom remembers that I used to crawl into her lap and say, "My head hurts," before I knew the word for what I felt. Our pediatrician told her I was too young for headaches. When I was nine, he blamed the pain on my personality; I was high strung with tinfoil nerves. In college, I took downers and smoked pot, and the headaches receded, or maybe I just forgot them. They reemerged the October after I moved to Santa Cruz. I was taking meeting minutes when a tingling pain calcified behind my eyes. "Does anyone have some Tylenol or morphine or something?" I said as we trickled out of a conference room. Ofelia gave me an Excedrin Migraine. The pain broke through it within 30 minutes. Brenda suggested I go to the ER. I felt ridiculous going to an emergency room for a headache, but I didn't know what else to do; I didn't have a doctor in California yet. The doctor I saw gave me eleven 7.5-milligram Vicodin. I took two and called the office. "I can come back," I told Brenda. She called me crazy. "Go home," she said. "Get some rest." I drove to my apartment in the mountains, curled up on the carpet, and took more Vicodin. I thought I'd save the rest, keep them around and get high a few times. But the migraine lasted seven days. I took all the pills and had the ER doctor call me in a refill. A month later, it happened again. In February, I got laid off and put on painkillers full time. By the time I left California to take a new job in D.C., I'd developed daily headaches, biweekly migraines, and a dependence on butalbital mixed with codeine.

7. When I tell people I'm taking opioids again, I say, "I thought about it a lot. It wasn't an easy decision." But I had already decided I wanted my opiates back before I walked into Piven's office, and I didn't think so much as I

worried about it. I still worry about it. I worry that when I leave Blacksburg I won't find a doctor to replace the one who writes my opioids now. I worry about the way I've yoked myself to a class of drugs so heavily scrutinized that some physicians refuse to dispense them at all, let alone to neurotic 30-year-old women who complain of invisible pain in their heads. I worry about whether I can make my prescription last the month that it's supposed to. I worry about my tolerance. I worry that eventually I'll require such a high dose just to make it through a regular day that I won't have the extra pills I need in order to write. I make contingency plans in my head: if I can't find another doctor, I tell myself, I'll find a methadone clinic. I'll do heroin. I'll buy pills from dealers. I'll be okay. But I don't know that. I'll only know that if something goes wrong, and I worry that it will.

8. In D.C., I swallowed butalbital with codeine like it was water. I probably ingested more pills than I did calories. I was the sole employee of a drug policy reform group that was really just an ugly website. My boss wanted me to update the news section by 8:00 a.m. Eastern even though most of the news then came out of California and Oregon. I woke up so early I couldn't hold down a real breakfast. I'd nibble on melon slices and gag over my toilet. I drank coffee until two in the afternoon, when I could hold down a Potbelly sub sandwich, the only thing in Dupont Circle that wasn't meat or pizza or fourteen dollars. I ate popcorn for dinner and smoked weed on my porch or in the beach chair in front of my TV. Aside from the tray the TV sat on and the beach chair and my mattress, I didn't have any furniture in my apartment. I called the mom at night. By then, I'd taken so many pills she could hear them in my slurred words. "The work you do… are you…?" she asked me once, and I said, "Yes, I'm stoned," because I preferred admitting to illegal drug use over telling the mom that I was high as fuck on prescription painkillers.

9. I don't tell the mom about the Opana. I tell her I've been taking oxycodone for about two weeks. Really, I spent three weeks snorting oxymorphone and then asked Piven to switch me down to oxycodone. I've been taking opioids again for a month when I tell the mom about them. I want to tell her while the pharmacist at Kroger refills my anti-anxiety pills, but I'm in public, and I know I'll cry when I do. I only called because it had been so long; I just wanted to say hi, check in. I don't need to call the mom again except that by the time the bus drops me off a block from my house I'm crying in that silent way that's more like choking because I've deceived the mom, and I know how much I'm about to disappoint her. I try to explain why it's different now. "I'm taking less in a day than I used to take in one pill," I say. She's not soothed. I get off the phone and feel worse. The mom is upset—maybe with me, maybe for me, maybe both and probably more—and I can't do anything about it. She calls me back a few minutes later and tells me she's sorry for getting mad. She says she trusts me and that she's just worried. I say I know; I'm scared, too. The mom says she isn't disappointed in me. She understands. I tell her I'm sorry anyway.

10. The mom told me once that I'm her favorite. She loves Beth and Chelsea; she likes them. But she likes me best. We're the most similar. We both worry too much. We're depressive and intense, and we need to talk about those feelings. We like mid-century junk and can't throw anything away. The mom keeps all our baby clothes and '80s toys in a storage unit with her American-flag fringe vest from the '70s and her sister's 1940s Brownie uniform. I keep her college notebooks on my writing desk, which was my great-grandmother's kitchen table. Every time I move to a new state, the dad says, "It would be cheaper just to buy new furniture." He doesn't understand the value the mom and I attach to hand-me-down chairs and vintage lamps. Stories and their props matter to us. The mom tells me stories she doesn't

always tell my sisters, like how she miscarried after she had us or what she really thinks about the dad's girlfriend. Last Christmas, she showed me a box full of old photos that the dad had told her to throw away after they got married. "I didn't," she said with a prim, proud smile. The pictures are of her old boyfriends. One is of her first husband, a geeky-looking Alabaman she married when she was nineteen and divorced before she turned 21. One is bearded; he looks at the camera, holding a Miller Lite and a fishing pole. He's not wearing a shirt. I joked that she should have married him instead. "He wasn't that kind of guy," she said, completely serious. One picture shows the mom riding shotgun in a prop plane. In another, she kicks her feet to stay afloat in the Gulf of Mexico; her hair fans out just beneath the water's blue-green surface, only her head and shoulders exposed to the air. The mom looks so pretty in these pictures. She's blond and thin as I am but with ample breasts and a big, candid smile. I can see why the dad didn't want her to keep 40-year-old snapshots of men who made her smile like that. But I can see, too, that she wants me to have pictures like these when I'm her age. She hopes I'll have stories as good as hers to tell and the love of men with beards and fishing poles. She wants me to live as full a life as she has, and if I'm on opioids, she isn't sure I can.

11. My mom texts me reassurance: *I know you'll be okay. Make sure to eat well and take care of yourself. I love you.* I can't compose a proper response. Every sentence I click out with my thumbs demands another. I'm still deleting and editing when she sends me a picture of Benny, our family's only surviving cat, sprawled across her bed. I'd slept there over my first winter and summer MFA breaks, which I spent away from Blacksburg. Benny acted like the mom's new bedroom was haunted. He'd stand at the threshold and meow when he wanted food in the middle of the night. We'd lift him from his favorite chair, set him between us on the bed, and pet him until he slunk back into the living room

as though he'd needed every muscle in his eighteen-year-old body to stay in the room for six minutes. *Benny now comes to the bed all the time*, the mom's text says. *His new favorite place.* I abort my reply and write a new one about how nice it is that Benny's come around to the bedroom. I add *Thanks* and *I love you, too* before I hit send.

12. The mom got a new bed when she moved out of her old house, so the bed I slept in when I last saw my mom was not the bed in which she lay depressed for a decade. It was not the bed in which I lay sweating and chattering my teeth and moaning about the pain in my stomach and my bones two years before I started taking opioids again. It was not the bed to which the mom brought soup and ice cream because they were the only things I could eat in withdrawal. When I wanted real food, she ordered me thin-crust Pizza Hut pizzas without cheese and let me eat them on sheets she didn't wash for two weeks because she knew that standing made me want to vomit. I hit week three and moved upstairs to Chelsea's old bed. I read Joyce Carol Oates and Barry Hannah and Amy Hempel's *Collected Stories* and all of *Infinite Jest* in the same rapacious, irritated way I'd binge-watched six seasons of *True Blood* and two of *Grey's Anatomy* and the entire run of *Weeds* in the mom's bed. When I held a book, my arm muscles twitched and quivered, and I'd wake up sore from wrist to wrist. I tried to write, but I couldn't sit up to type without feeling nauseated and feverish. I would leave for Virginia in a week, and I still wasn't strong enough to do anything but shuffle around the mom's house, in and out of beds in which no one sleeps anymore.

13. I used to call the mom's old house "our" house, but the dad abandoned his claim on it when he left with nothing but his clothes. He moved into a furnished condo on the Destin Harbor, the opposite of the big house on the

Choctawhatchee Bay that the mom dictated to an architect when my sisters and I were in third grade. She filled it with junk-shop antiques and the furniture we inherited from the dad's grandmother. He didn't want any of that, nothing from his old life. The only thing he's asked for since he moved out is the Kinks box set that Beth, Chelsea, and I gave him on the last Christmas the parents spent together. I saw it sitting beside the mom's new front door when I rolled my suitcase in from the airport last summer. "He didn't even want his Kinks box set?" I asked. Usually, when the dad opens a present, he says, "It's a nice... a nice... tie" or "a nice... a nice... book." You can tell he's underwhelmed. But, after he opened the box set, I took a video of the dad running his finger over the *Picture Book* track list and singing the first few lines of 138 Kinks songs. The mom said he'd called to ask if I could bring it to him when we met for dinner on Thursday. "I'm hauling around 20 years of a life, and he walks away with some suits and CDs," she said. I didn't tell her it hurt my feelings that he hadn't missed the box set sooner.

14. The first time a guy broke up with me, the mom took me into the closet under the stairs where she kept her records. We sat cross-legged on the carpet and flipped through Harry Chapin and Bob Dylan; Graham Parsons and Hank Williams; The Doors, The Beatles, The Rolling Stones. "All the cheesy ones are your dad's," the mom said as she passed over Rod Stewart and pulled out a stack of Emmylou Harris albums. "I always listened to her when I was sad," she told me. I took the records up to my room and listened to *Luxury Liner* first because the mom said it was her favorite. I put on *Quarter Moon in a Ten Cent Town* because I liked the title and then *Elite Hotel* because Emmylou looked so cool and tough on the cover. I listened for echoes of the mom's sadness and of my own. I imagined my mother at sixteen, horizontal beside a record player in the suede miniskirt I keep in my closet now and the

lace-up boots whose soles I broke when I tried to move them to New York. I understood then that my mom had invited me to know her in a way she'd never done before. I'm sure she also gave me advice and told me I'd feel better with time, but I only remember the way she handed me those records and inducted me into a fellowship of broken-hearted women. When we talk about opioids, we talk about a heartbreak more cutting than any a lover could inflict. The words we use with men are bloodless compared to the empathy and fury the mom and I yell over each other on the days when she's sick of hearing about my pills and I'm sick of other people interfering in my health. We have our own language for it, but we can't teach it to you. Our fellowship is too exclusive, the cost of entry too high.

15. The dad and I don't talk about my headaches. When I lived in New York and had little else to talk about, he'd tell me he wasn't interested if our phone conversations veered into headache territory. But we must have talked about them at dinner the night before I moved to Virginia. I don't remember what I said, but I remember the dad's reply: "Well, I wouldn't have taken the pills in the first place," he said. He'd just paid the check. I said, "Yes, you would have." To hear him tell it, the dad's pain tops the charts, and when it strikes, he's the first to reach for a bottle of Aleve, a tube of Gold Bond cream, a carton of Epsom salt. The dad takes pride in his self-sufficiency. He doesn't want to admit to his mortality, to consider that one day his own body will hurt in ways he can't endure. That he might bow to an addictive drug scares him too much to contemplate. So, the dad's story about my headaches has something to do with a weakness in me: I was in pain, and I took the easy way out.

16. The mom doesn't like me taking opioids again because she knows it isn't easy. She's heard me complain about stingy doctors and out-of-stock pharmacies

and the side effects that render most headache prophylactics untenable; she knows how many things I've tried and that none have worked. The dad thinks, if he thinks about it at all, that getting on and then off opioids was easy for me because I made it look easy. He has the luxury of thinking that way because he didn't have to see it. But the mom watched me lose the ten pounds I haven't gained back; she can see that I don't have ten more pounds to lose. She understands that opiate withdrawal increased my anxiety to the point that I still take what psychiatrists consider the "ceiling dose" for Klonopin. She knows because she paid for it when I didn't have any money left that I can't afford another Suboxone detox. That I might never get off opioids again upsets the mom in part because she thinks it means I've given up. "Just don't give up," she says each time I see a new doctor or try a new treatment. "I won't," I say, but I have. Last month, a pain specialist phoned Audrey, my primary care physician, to warn her that I'm not really a pain patient because I wouldn't let him inject lidocaine and cortisol into my occipital nerve. "The idea is," Audrey explained the next time I saw her, "that if you were really in pain, you'd try absolutely anything to make it stop." Since I'd said no to the injections, the pain doctor decided that I just wanted drugs. I sat next to Audrey and cried. I told her that the other doctor was right. I do want drugs. I know drugs work, and I'm tired of getting my hopes up over miracle cures that never materialize.

17. The dad actually left the mom twice. I can't know for sure, but I think he went back to her because he talked to a lawyer and realized how much money a divorce would cost him. He went back to his marriage the way I've gone back to opiates: in stages, tentative and brazen. He tested his resolve one last time, but his effort lacked conviction. And when he decided he'd had enough of trying, he told the mom he didn't want a divorce this time. He didn't want to involve lawyers. He would give her a monthly allowance and let her remain

on his health insurance plan. She could keep the house. On paper they'd be married but would live separate lives in different places. He got the idea from his girlfriend, who'd made the same arrangement with her husband. The mom insisted on a real divorce. "I have to look out for myself," she said. I said I was proud of her. I said she was right. I pictured her old and infirm, the dad unwilling or unable to take care of her the way she took care of him and his house and his children for three decades. "You shouldn't have to depend on him," I said. I know that when the mom expresses her apprehension about opioids, she's telling me the same thing: she doesn't want my life to revolve around doctors and pills again; she doesn't want me to depend on drugs the way the dad asked her to depend on him. "I won't let it get that bad," I promise her. But I might.

18. When I stopped taking oxys and got off Suboxone for good, my mom and my sisters and my friends and my doctor in New York all said they were *so proud* of me. I hated hearing people say they were proud of me. I didn't achieve anything. I did what I had to do, what I was supposed to do, what I thought I should do. It was hard but not because I craved opiates; I craved pain relief. Suboxone is mostly buprenorphine, a partial opioid agonist. Partial agonists don't activate as many of the brain's natural opioid receptors as do full agonists (codeine, oxycodone, morphine, heroin), but they offer some analgesic effects. Doctors drew me pictures and used elaborate analogies, but until I took it, I didn't understand how Suboxone would work. I didn't expect it to provide any pain relief at all. When I habituated to it and found my headaches kind of bearable, I thought the full agonists I'd been taking had actually caused the pain, and I blamed myself for it. I didn't feel proud, and it embarrassed me that anyone thought I ought to. When I tell the mom I'm taking opiates again, I want her to be proud of me for trying to stay off of

them and proud of me for recognizing that I can't. I want her to be proud of me for being honest with her, and I want her to be proud of me the way I'm proud of myself: I made the decision I needed to make even though I knew it would disappoint everyone I loved, even though I knew exactly how hard enacting that decision and meeting those needs would be.

19. The mom says I was a different person when I downed 300 milligrams of oxycodone every day, and she doesn't want me to be that person again. I wish I could see what she saw. I never told her about the way I used to cross Flatbush Avenue at rush hour, muttering "Go ahead" to cars I nearly let hit me, so I don't know if, when she calls me *different*, she's referring to the way the pain and the energy I exerted trying to alleviate it left me sunken and scraped up like my knees the summer I broke my only flat sandals and tripped so often in five-inch wedges that I still have scars where then I had scabs. The mom tells me that the pills make me negative and angry and single-minded. Mostly, I think that's what she means by *different*. But she might mean something else. I'm afraid to ask. Sometimes I think my mom loves me in spite of the drugs I take, and that's what really scares me. She accepts that I need opioids, but she's not happy about it. The way the mom feels about opioids parallels the rhetoric of tolerance: we don't like what you do, but we'll live with it; hate the sin, love the sinner. I tried to explain one night how I've thrived during this year I've spent taking opioids again. But, for the mom, oxycodone remains an unfortunate drug I have to use because no one knows why I have headaches or how to stop them. She knows how much of my life pain obliterates, but I can't make her see how much more I lose if I don't have the pills that take it away.

20. Every time I see my psychiatrist at the student health center, I fill out a form that asks me whether I have *thoughts of ending my life*. I always click

the *0* that means *not at all like me*. But I'm at least kind of lying. I'm 30 years old, and every morning I take a blood pressure pill, an anti-anxiety drug, and an opioid. Of course I've thought about it. I answer *0* because I don't think about ending my life in the way the question means. I look at my life and wonder if preserving it is worth all this effort. I don't imagine what I'd write in the note or all the ways I could do it and how each one might fail; I don't imagine killing myself at all. I don't even really think about how I'll die (I already know: I smoke, and I've been killing my liver since I could open a child-proof Tylenol bottle). I picture the next 30, 40, 50 years and wonder how I'll bear them, what shape they'll take, if I'll still be able to write and what I'll do when I can't; I think about why I want to live. When I tell my mom I'm taking opioids again, I'm telling her how I will.

PRODUCT WARNING

PATIENT PRESCRIPTION INFORMATION

Mickelson, David   12/16/02
1402 19th Street
Niceville, FL 32578
Ph: 850.533.0592   Refills: 0

METHADONE 10 MG TABLETS
TAKE 1 TABLET BY MOUTH TWICE DAILY

This is an OVAL-shaped, WHITE TABLET imprinted with 54 142 on the front.
METHADONE - ORAL – (METH a done)

USES: I didn't ask David why he had methadone pills when he'd told me that a nurse watched him drink his methadone at the clinic every morning. I didn't know yet that David bought or had doctors prescribe him extra opiates because the clinic dose didn't get him high. And despite what he said, David really just wanted to get high. I guess it occurred to me, and I guess I didn't care. I had never been high, and I had never wanted to get high. People ask what drew me to David back then or what compelled me to take methadone when I'd never even been stoned. I can't answer them. Except maybe to say that David was 22 and looked like a cross between Conor Oberst and Kurt Cobain, and when—at eighteen—I said I'd never been high, I knew I sounded silly and young and boring to his ears.

HOW TO USE: I should have been scared, but I wasn't. I don't know why. Probably an OVAL-shaped, WHITE TABLET felt safe. A pharmacist in a clean white jacket dispenses OVAL-shaped, WHITE TABLETS; a doctor prescribes them. The night I got high for the first time, David removed three OVAL-shaped, WHITE TABLETS from a translucent orange bottle with his name on it. His name on that bottle sanctioned those pills. He gave one to me and took two for himself.

SIDE EFFECTS: I swallowed my pill and 20 minutes later emerged as a pool of warm, scratchy light. I wasn't silly or young or boring anymore. When I talked, I knew I had a right to what I said. I don't remember what I said. What I said didn't matter. It only mattered that I said it, that I wasn't the girl who'd sat mute and dumb when David propped his feet up on my dash that first day and told me all about his heroin addiction and his dead girlfriend and his move back to Destin from New York City. I didn't feel self-conscious and awkward the way I'd felt around David when I said I'd never been high. High, I felt electric and brilliant. I felt like a badass. But I can't say that I took methadone because I wanted to feel like an electric, brilliant badass; I didn't know how opioids would make me feel until I took one. I don't think I'd even considered it. I think I started doing drugs because I wanted a boy to like me.

DRUG INTERACTIONS: We took the methadone, and then David and I snorted cocaine he cut into big lines on a desk in the half-finished apartment above his dad's auto shop, where he lived when I first knew him. I don't remember wondering why we were doing cocaine when David had told me three days earlier that he wanted to get clean. Post-cocaine, my memory splices a few individual frames into an otherwise blank reel. I remember lying with David on the floor, neck bent so my chin stuck in the air; he said the coke would hit harder if I let it drip straight into my throat. I remember tracing with my index finger the skull-and-crossbones tattoo on his wrist, but that might have been another time. Mostly, I remember standing in Walmart cashing a check so we could buy more coke. I don't remember how I felt the first time I did cocaine, but I know because I wrote the check that I wanted to feel it more.

OVERDOSE: 100-pound girls shouldn't take drugs from basically strange men. But opiated and coked up, I felt safe because I'd been careless. I mimicked David's cocky saunter and decided I would be, should be, maybe always had been someone else. Someone else might have been smarter about mixing a central nervous system depressant with a stimulant; I had no tolerance at all, and adding an upper to a downer put stress on my unsuspecting heart. But that night David didn't feel like a stranger, and I didn't know about tolerances and bad chemical combinations, so I couldn't die.

PATIENT PRESCRIPTION INFORMATION

Mickelson, David   01/13/03
1402 19th St.
Niceville, FL 32601
Ph: 850.533.0592   Refills: 1 before 01/13/04

ALPRAZOLAM 2 MG TABLETS
TAKE 1 CAPSULE BY MOUTH THREE TIMES DAILY

This is a WHITE, OBLONG-shaped, MULTI-SCORED TABLET imprint-
ed with R039 on the front.
ALPRAZOLAM - ORAL – (al PRAY zoe lam)
COMMON BRAND NAME(S): Xanax

USES: When I asked him how it would feel, David said Xanax would relax
me. He started taking it for panic attacks, which is the only true thing I ever
heard him tell a doctor. But he took it so often—just to relax, just because he
could—that, when panic struck, his heart wouldn't stop racing and his palm
wouldn't stop throbbing unless he took three or four times his prescribed dose.
I'd never had a panic attack, but I believed David when he said I needed to relax.

HOW TO USE: On our first date, David crushed up a Xanax bar with his ID
and a cassette-tape case on the center console of my 1997 Chrysler Intrepid.
He divided the powder into two lines and sniffed one up his nose through a
rolled-up dollar bill. I thought the Xanax would be sticky like the coke, so I
inhaled too hard. I coughed and held my thumb against my burning nostril in
case all the powder spewed out when I exhaled too hard, too.

SIDE EFFECTS: I remember that touching my own hair felt like petting an expensive stuffed toy—a bunny or some other animal whose simulacra it seems necessary to make light and pillowy. David and I walked down the block hand in hand, and our skin like worn-in cotton. We saw a movie called *Narc*. *Narc* opened in late 2002 and did so poorly at the box office that it released straight to the cheap second-run theater where David and I saw it. I don't remember a single thing about the movie except that the scenes were dark and the plot had something to do with the DEA. I kept leaning over to ask David what had happened and who was who until the credits rolled without warning. "What?" I said. "That movie was, like, five minutes long." After the novelty wore off, Xanax quit turning me plush-doll soft and disoriented. I just felt relaxed the way David said I would. But we never relaxed about Xanax; if David didn't have any, the withdrawal could induce seizures. He could die. He'd been on it for years.

DRUG INTERACTIONS: I used Xanax to potentiate other drugs and to come down from cocaine highs. I took it after near catastrophes, like if David got ripped off by a dealer or couldn't get a new opioid prescription when he needed one, and he always needed one. Sometimes the near catastrophe was a fight. David liked to fuck with me. He'd tell me he'd cheated or contracted HIV or pretend to be possessed by a demon; he threatened to tell my parents that I hadn't stopped seeing him like they'd insisted but had actually let him move with me to Gainesville, where we were right then getting high in a motel room for which his mother paid. I believed everything, even his *Exorcist* impressions, until he laughed and told me he'd made it all up. Sometimes he waited until I believed that, too, and said he'd lied about lying. I'd get mad, and then I'd cry, and David would console me as if he had the right. I don't know why I let him or why I put up with it except that David said he loved me, and I said I loved him, too. At nineteen, I knew that real love was intense and dramatic. You were supposed to cry.

OVERDOSE: All the time David would pile too much Xanax on top of too many opiates and nod out. Usually it was nothing: his head drooped, and his cigarette burned streaks into my car's upholstery or holes in his shirts or our sheets. Nod, blink, repeat. Other times he stopped breathing, and I had to shake him back to life. More than once, he told me he'd woken up to a slap from his mother, who'd found him overdosing in his motel room. When I couldn't get him on the phone, I just knew he'd died. Even now, when someone doesn't answer my calls, I picture them dead.

PATIENT PRESCRIPTION INFORMATION

Long, Amy   01/09/04
45 Springs Residential Complex
Gainesville, FL 32601
Ph: 850.582.4074   Refills: 0

HYDROCODONE-CHLORPHENIRAMINE
7.5–500 MG/15 ML SYRUP
TAKE 5 ML EVERY TWELVE HOURS

This is a YELLOW SYRUP.
HYDROCODONE-CHLORPHENIRAMINE - ORAL –
(HYE droe KOE done - KLOR fen IR a meen)
COMMON BRAND NAME(S): Tussionex

USES: David told doctors that a car he'd been working under fell on him and pinched his sciatic nerve. He'd say he was new to town and needed someone to write his painkillers until an appointment opened up at the pain management clinic, where they'd run tests and take scans and find nothing wrong with his back. The first time I shopped a doctor, I didn't need a story. I actually exhibited the symptoms for which Tussionex is indicated: nasal congestion, sore throat, body aches, a cough so savage it left my ribs sore. "Last time I had this, my doctor gave me… I think it was called Tussionex?" I said like someone who couldn't recite the periodic table of opiates off the top of her head. When I met David in the parking lot, I waved my prescription like a captured flag.

HOW TO USE: We passed the amber plastic bottle between us on the drive back to our room at the Gainesville Motor Lodge. David unlocked the door and lit a cigarette. I'd cut back to preserve my throat, but I had a fresh codeine buzz and the sugary syrup coating my tongue, so I took one, too, and curled up under the rarely washed blanket. Even on Tussionex, I didn't feel like getting out of bed, but David had friends in town and wanted to take them out that night. "Don't make me look like a jackass," he said and said until I walked downtown with him anyway. The bouncer at Dirty Nelly's waved me off; I wasn't 21. I faked disappointment and walked back to the motel alone, eager to slip out of my jeans and into our bed's cheap, stiff sheets.

SIDE EFFECTS: The bars had been closed for over an hour when David stumbled drunk into our room with a girl I didn't know. He flicked on a lamp. I snapped at him to turn it off. The girl was dressed and primped, and it didn't seem fair that she should see me in my pajamas, unwashed and ugly with a cold. "I told Tara she could use our bathroom," David said, as if her full bladder rendered the rest of her body benign. I'd have described Tara as chubby, maybe because her curves made me look like a twelve-year-old boy. She was a cherubic sort of cute. Moon face. Pert nose and anime eyes. Pixie cut dyed a pinkish-red hue. She moved too comfortably in our room, not bothered enough that I was there. David and I whispered to each other while Tara pissed, and he took too long to walk her to her car. "On your side," I said when he climbed into bed fully clothed.

DRUG INTERACTIONS: In the morning, I told David I'd be back in an hour. I spent it just sitting in the dorm room I never used, pretending to think. I returned exactly when I'd said I would and found Tara and her friend Tammy eating ninety-nine-cent burritos at the foot of our bed. They were both too friendly. Their voices chirped. David said they'd dropped by, that he didn't invite them. I said David and I needed to talk and kicked them out. Tara invited us over to her place to get stoned and play Mario Kart when we finished, as if she didn't know what I needed to talk to David about. Or maybe she knew exactly and so knew, too, that her invitation already excluded me.

OVERDOSE: David cursed and pleaded and painted impossible white picket fences into our future. He grabbed at threads the way he'd done once with my checkbook when I wouldn't pay $175 so he could see a pill-mill doctor in Ocala. He cried. Actual tears. "I *need* you," he said. If he could make me feel guilty, I might change my mind; I'd done it before. But now I had Tara. Tara was concrete, something to which I could point and say, "That." I pointed until David gave up. He put on his shoes and asked me to drive him to Tara's house. "I could use to get stoned and play Mario Kart," he said. I kissed him for what I said would be the last time and dropped him on his new girlfriend's doorstep.

PATIENT PRESCRIPTION INFORMATION

Mickelson, David   03/06/04
1100 SW 8th Ave
Gainesville, FL 32601
Ph: 352.718.0363   Refills: 0

OXYCODONE HCI/APAP 5/500 MG CAPSULE
TAKE 1–2 CAPSULES BY MOUTH AS NEEDED FOR PAIN

This is a RED/WHITE, CAPSULE-shaped CAPSULE imprinted with 54
392 on the side.
OXYCODONE HCI/APAP - ORAL –
(OX I KOE done and a SEET a MIN oh fen)
COMMON BRAND NAME(S): Tylox

USES: David went back on the methadone clinic, but Tara wouldn't drive him there. He took the bus or begged rides from me. When he could afford it, David bought pills from other patients on the clinic steps. When he couldn't, he subsisted on his methadone and the odd prescription from a dentist who'd once written him a bunch of Percocet for some gnarly tooth infection. The third time he complained that the tooth still bothered him, Dr. Smiles switched David from Percocet to Tylox. Tylox is oxycodone cut with way too much acetaminophen. The pills were weak and dirty, but David did what he could with what he could get.

HOW TO USE: Tara learned to use what she could get, too, except all she could get was me. I'd take David to the clinic or to fill his Tylox prescriptions, then sit on the futon in his new apartment and watch him open RED/WHITE, CAPSULE-shaped CAPSULES, pour their powder onto his kitchenette counter, and snort piles of gold-ish granules every ten minutes because that's about how long a Tylox high lasts. I drew the line at putting 500 milligrams of acetaminophen up my own nose.

SIDE EFFECTS: David and I got along better when we weren't dating. I remembered why I'd liked him in the first place. He was familiar. He knew what I meant when I told stories about watching my friends skateboard at the Landing or going to shows in church basements after the Java Pit closed. I had heard rumors about his friends, and he'd heard rumors about mine. He talked to me in a way no one else in Gainesville could because we had the same touchstones. He made me laugh. He gave unbeatable head. David and I never had penetrative sex while we were a couple, and we didn't have it when we cheated on Tara, either. He swore he never shared needles, but I was too smart now to bet my life on what David said. Besides, I'd shared all my other below-the-waist firsts with him. I wanted to experience my last first with someone new.

DRUG INTERACTIONS: David winked at his penis when he wanted me to go down on him. The wink wasn't funny or sexy; it erased any desire I had to so much as approach his dick. He thought he could change my mind if his fingers or tongue hit the right spots, but the second I felt myself about to come, I pushed him off me. "I can't do this," I'd say, and David would groan as though Tara were actually my girlfriend, my problem. But the problem wasn't only Tara. I knew I was doing the wrong thing. I think I kept doing it to prove I hadn't been rejected, that David still wanted me. But I'd seen what he could offer and said I didn't want it. I'd rejected him. For two months I hovered on the verge of an orgasm I felt too guilty and confused to achieve. David hardly ever finished either, but he didn't act like it mattered much. He put on his clothes, turned his back to me, and pulled apart another Tylox.

OVERDOSE: I don't remember how Tara found out. Maybe she walked in on us. Maybe someone told her, but I don't know who could have. Probably David said something. Maybe he wanted to make Tara jealous, or maybe it started as a joke and she saw through it. Maybe David did to Tara the same things he'd done to me, and maybe she stopped at angry and never moved into sad. I don't know. I wasn't there (unless I was). The next time she saw me, Tara poured her beer on my head from the second-floor alcove at the University Club, a gay bar where we danced to The Smiths and The Strokes and The Cure on Monday nights. I guess I deserved it, but I went upstairs and called her a cunt anyway. "What did you think would happen?" I asked. "He cheated on me with you."

PATIENT PRESCRIPTION INFORMATION

Mickelson, David   08/24/04
1100 SW 8th Ave
Gainesville, FL 32601
Ph: 850.533.0592   Refills: 1 before 02/24/05

HYDROCODONE-APAP 7.5/300 MG TABLETS
TAKE 1 TABLET BY MOUTH THREE TIMES DAILY

This is a WHITE, OVAL-shaped, SCORED TABLET imprinted with M358 on the front.
HYDROCODONE-APAP - ORAL –
(hye droe KOE done and a SEET a MIN oh fen)
COMMON BRAND NAME(S): Vicodin, Lortab, Norco

USES: David said he'd seen "NO NARCOTICS" scrawled on top of his chart at the university hospital, but he kept trying its emergency room anyway, and sometimes he left with a prescription. He still used the herniated disc story and the recent move excuse even though he'd lived in Gainesville for almost a year. If a doctor noticed all his ER visits and asked why David still hadn't seen a pain specialist, he put his head in his hands and cited unemployment and uninsurability. You could believe it if you wanted to, and David made you want to. I assume he brought Tara into exam rooms with him the way he'd brought me. We were props, as effective as his fake hobble. We spoke well and kept our hair neat and went to college. We looked like nice girls, like the kinds of girls who don't date junkies.

HOW TO USE: I only know what David told me. He said he'd miscalculated his pharmacy schedule and brought his prescription to a CVS he'd used two weeks earlier. Florida didn't have a prescription-drug monitoring program then, so pharmacists flagged patients they suspected of doctor shopping. CVS suspected David, and one of its techs called the police. The cops interrogated Tara, and it scared her. I don't think she really knew what David was doing. She talked about his drug use as an annoyance or an endearing quirk but not as something illegal. Maybe she thought David's prescriptions were legitimate because doctors wrote them; she might not have known that he was obligated to tell each one what the others did. Either way, Tara decided that David wasn't worth risking a criminal record. She could handle infidelity, but she dumped him when he got arrested.

SIDE EFFECTS: Alachua County charged David with concealing information to obtain a controlled substance and sentenced him to six months in jail. Tara wouldn't visit, so I did. We sat on steel benches and cracked barbed jokes at the other's expense into black plastic phones. David laughed when other inmates hit on me. "Come see me, baby," they'd call over concrete-block partitions. I teased them back, said "Next time." We made fun of Tara's innocence and pretended it had never been mine. I felt safer, less reckless with a plexiglass wall between us. I didn't worry about how David would get his Xanax or stave off opiate withdrawal. And he couldn't touch me, so we couldn't fall back into old, bad patterns.

DRUG INTERACTIONS: Before she knew that David and I had fucked around behind her back, Tara considered us friends. I think she felt guilty about interrupting my relationship, and I felt sorry for her, four years older than I was and with no better sense. She left beers in bathroom stalls for me to chug, and I offered up my David expertise. But now we were enemies. When she changed her mind and started visiting him in jail, David and I planned my trips so Tara would never know about them. The schedule got so complicated that I let her take it over. David receded into my background. Tara picked him up when the county released him at midnight in February.

OVERDOSE: Tara wanted David to get clean, and he kept doing the same shit. After they broke up, David was at my house all the time. He came over and distracted me when I told him I needed to work. He stole weed from the container I kept perpetually stocked on my coffee table and palmed any money I left out in the open. He woke me up at six in the morning, banging on my windows like I'd already agreed to drive him to the methadone clinic. When I told him I didn't want him in my house anymore, David shoved open the door I blocked with my body and entered anyway. I wasn't strong enough to stop him, and I was too embarrassed to admit I was scared. I got tougher. I got better at saying no. But I couldn't shake the feeling that I owed him some kind of care.

PATIENT PRESCRIPTION INFORMATION

Long, Amy   11/30/06
1113 SW 4th Ave
Gainesville, FL 32601
Ph: 850.582.4074   Refills: 1 before 05/30/08

CLONAZEPAM 1 MG TABLETS
TAKE 1 TABLET BY MOUTH AS NEEDED FOR ANXIETY

This is a ROUND, WHITE, SCORED TABLET imprinted with R 34 on the front.
CLONAZEPAM - ORAL – (kloe NAZ e pam)
COMMON BRAND NAME(S): Klonopin

USES: I remember exactly the episode of *Grey's Anatomy* I was watching when my heart started racing and wouldn't stop. I knew I'd die; the muscle would give out or crack open my ribcage. I drove myself to the ER at Shands—I could see it from my house—ticking off cardiovascular disorders on my car's steering wheel. The nurse who did my EKG told me that, yes, this could be a heart attack. When I saw the doctor, he didn't see anything wrong with my heart. He told me I'd had a panic attack and wrote me a prescription for a dozen Xanax.

HOW TO USE: I didn't want to take Xanax forever (it's too short-acting, too easily addicting), and somehow I knew I would take the pills I got that night for the rest of my life. I went to a doctor David used to see and told him I'd rather take Klonopin. I didn't think of what I did as doctor shopping or of myself as imitating David. I simply knew this doctor would write me what I asked for and wouldn't stop writing it unless I stopped asking.

SIDE EFFECTS: David would have stolen my Klonopin, too, but by then he wasn't legally allowed within 500 feet of me. At the courthouse, I didn't know how to fill out the forms. David and I weren't married or dating; he'd never physically hurt me. I said he'd tried to break into my house. I didn't say that after he did I drove him to the methadone clinic. The police took almost a week to serve David with the papers, and until David had seen and signed the papers, the restraining order didn't mean anything. He was never home. I didn't know where or if he worked. He knocked on my door once, sat smoking at my picnic table to see if I'd come out. He didn't know about the papers or that if I talked to him I'd void my own request for protection. I dropped to my knees and crawled across the hardwood floors so David wouldn't see me. The 911 operator didn't seem to register the urgency in my voice or understand what I meant when I whispered that I needed an officer to serve my ex-boyfriend with an injunction. By the time a refrigerator-chested cop ambled over holding no papers, David was gone.

DRUG INTERACTIONS: Once, I sat right beside him on my weed dealer's couch and didn't even know until David said, "This is a lot closer than 500 feet." He'd buzzed his hair, packed on ten or fifteen new pounds. But his voice hadn't changed. I bolted up off my seat. "You have to leave," I said. "You can't be here." David said that sounded like Jimmy's decision. Jimmy didn't want to get involved. We all knew I wouldn't call the police. Another time, David had his friend Gideon call me and ask after him. Gideon and David sound like twins: same nasal voice, Northwest Florida accent, heroin slur. "If I didn't know better," I said a few minutes in, "I'd swear you were David." David said, "I am, idiot." Gideon had passed him the phone.

OVERDOSE: I used to get sick when semesters ended, like my body knew I couldn't afford a week in bed until I'd finished all my papers. I didn't think about my panic attacks that way until I started writing about David nearly ten years later, searching the county court website for dates I needed to know. I filed for the injunction in April. Gideon called in August. That episode of *Grey's Anatomy* aired on Thanksgiving, when I thought David and I were really over. But maybe listening for his footsteps in my yard and keeping tabs on everything in my house and hiding from him in Publix because I didn't know the rules that governed public places put more stress on me than I knew. Maybe I didn't know how scared and angry a person I'd become, how brittle. Maybe I thought I was dealing with it when I wasn't. Maybe my body rebelled against the responsibility I felt for an adult man who'd uprooted his shit life to be near his teenage girlfriend and then replaced her four months later. Maybe the too-fast beat of my heart attested to what I didn't know how else to say.

INITIATION

1. The first time I saw David, I think my mouth hung open like a cartoon dog's. He seemed more like a mirage than a real person, a trick the sharp December sun played on the silver asphalt. I watched him cross the Santa Rosa Mall parking lot beside a gangly friend. I rode my brakes and circled back around so I could stare at him. I didn't think anyone looked like that outside of Hollywood. The day I met him, David had on a camel-colored suede jacket over a white Hanes T-shirt. The jacket's sleeves were knit like a sweater, and each had a suede patch sewn onto its elbow. I noticed the patches when David lifted his arm to brush his bangs from his deep-set brown eyes. He wore his brown hair in a long sort of crew cut, and it flopped into his eyes when he lowered his head to laugh. When he smiled, the sun hit his incisors and made him look like a big cat. David walked with this sloping, dopey saunter that seemed at odds with his jaguar posture and the way he tilted his chin toward the sky. He disappeared through the mall's glass doors, that teasing leonine grin still spread across his face. I parked and checked my appearance in my rearview mirror. I didn't expect to see David again, but I wanted to know how I'd look if I did.

2. My sisters and I spent our last two years of high school at a public charter school on the Okaloosa-Walton Community College campus. Some of our friends from the bigger high school transferred with us, and we knew a few

people who'd graduated and were taking general education classes there. The dozen of us comprised a clearly defined group in our Chuck Taylors and black T-shirts. We sat on a certain picnic table in the grassy campus center and shit-talked each other all day. Ahmed and Eric practiced landing ollies on a wheel-less skateboard deck. Our friend Jason strummed a miniature guitar; when we walked to our cars for illicit off-campus lunches at KFC or Wendy's and any time one of us approached the home-base bench, his spaghetti-Western folk soundtracks plotted our movements. Mike Daley was our "bad" friend; he smoked cigarettes. I'd never done anything worse than cut a class to make out with my boyfriend in his van. Other kids—the band nerds and the home-schoolers from DeFuniak and Crestview—had actual sex in the woods behind the theater building. One girl got pregnant. But we didn't do that stuff. We got good grades. We went to youth group on weeknights. We watched our friends' Christian punk bands play in the fellowship halls of various local churches or at the Java Pit, an all-ages venue in Fort Walton that the dad hated; after it closed, we'd stand outside The Point, a bar that hosted bands in its place, and watch the shows through a fishbowl window. The parents worried about us loitering downtown. They worried about my bright-red hair and weird friends with piercings and opposite-gender haircuts. They worried when Leah stole her parents' Volvo and tried to run away from home; she and Chelsea's best friend Rebecca drove in circles around Fairhope, Alabama, until a cop pulled them over and cuffed their thin wrists to a bench in the police station. Leah's parents picked them up in the morning. The mom worried each time she drove us to Pensacola so we could see Hot Water Music play at Sluggo's, but she still let us pile out of the car a few blocks from the venue door. The parents must have known they were lucky to have my sisters and me. We were such good kids. And then I wasn't.

3. I don't know any more why I'd driven to the mall after school that day. I think I had a purpose, but whatever it was, I didn't put much effort into fulfilling it. I remember maybe needing to return a pair of jeans to The Gap. Maybe David came with me, or maybe I ran the errand alone. I know I stopped to talk to Jack, a barista at the Coffee Beanery who had a crush on my sister Chelsea; his sister Christina had been David's first girlfriend. David and the gangly friend he walked in with, whom I recognized up close as Josh Gordon, had been a few years ahead of Jack at Rocky Bayou Christian School. The three of them made a loose triangle at the marble counter. I froze. I didn't know if I should walk away from or toward them. I didn't know who David was, but Josh and his two brothers were notorious in the local punk scene. I didn't really know why; I'd just heard they were rough guys. One of them had played college football. Jack waved at me, said my name. I stepped forward, one foot on the Coffee Beanery's tile floor. "I'll come back," I said. "You're busy." But David stopped me. He bought my cappuccino, which I ordered because it was the only fancy coffee drink I could name. I know David flirted with me, but I don't remember how. It didn't matter. Whatever way he flirted, I would have swooned. David says he fell for me right then, but I don't believe it. I looked like a wet rat all through my teen years. I was stick thin and flat chested, and I hadn't yet figured out how or what it meant to embrace my body's shape. I could never find jeans that fit. The smallest sizes sagged on me like their seats were hammocks my ass had abandoned. The day I met David, I had on a unisex T-shirt I'd bought in September when I dragged Ahmed with me to see Tori Amos on her *Scarlet's Walk* tour. I'd tied a navy-blue bandana over my blood-red hair. I was growing out a too-short spring cut, and the bandana was supposed to cover my mullet. I can't name a single thing that should have attracted David to me. Sometimes I think he sensed that I was insecure and naïve and wanted someone to pay me *that* kind of

attention. Every time I ask, David tells me I'm wrong, that I looked striking, and I don't know what to think. We are both unreliable narrators. When I ask him about the first time he saw me, David doesn't always remember that Josh was there, but if Josh hadn't said he needed to leave and David that he wanted to stay, I wouldn't have said I'd drive David home; without Josh, the story falls apart. We both remember that David asked me to go with him to FYE, a chain store that boasted double-digit rows of new and used CDs, a wall of Bob Marley and Pink Floyd posters, stereo equipment on cork-board shelves. Of course I said yes. We waved to Jack. I shook Josh's hand. David and I walked to the other side of the mall, entering FYE through the double-door-sized opening cut into its glass walls. I flipped through stacks of CDs without pausing, too insecure to admit my own taste in music. David pried open jewel cases and slipped the discs into the waistband of his boxer shorts. I didn't know he'd done it until he put his hand down his pants and spread the gleaming haul on my passenger seat. There were lots of things I didn't know about David then. He was a stranger. And still I turned my key in my car's ignition and locked myself in beside him.

4. When I met David, I had relatively recently turned eighteen and relatively recently been dumped. Willy, my first real boyfriend, had broken up with me at the end of eleventh grade. He parked in my parents' driveway, sat me down on the side of his powder-blue Astro Van, and listed all the reasons our relationship no longer made sense. Willy's calm, matter-of-fact delivery carried the weight of fact, as though I were objectively undateable, if not unloveable. Willy insisted he still cared about me. He wanted to remain friends, he said, good ones, and I shouldn't read his rejection as a verdict passed on my worth as a person or a woman or even a romantic prospect. My sisters and most of our friend group had intimated for years that I was ridiculous, the butt of

some eternal joke no one bothered to explain to me. The joke had something to do with my inclination toward introspection and solitude, with the serious way I approached my identity and interpreted the world. The joke referenced an intensity that manifested itself in the leg I shook up and down when I sat, in my hands that never stilled, in the wrinkle that etched itself into my forehead before I'd turned sixteen. I was weird—and not the good, punk-rock weird to which Taylor staked claim with her blue hair and septum piercing. I was too earnest and faced too far inward; I was too wide-eyed, too romantic, and yet also too hard. In pictures, I appear off-kilter in my body, which makes me look vulnerable but cagey, like a feral kitten. My visible collarbone advertises how easily I might snap, but my bent elbows look sharp and mean. My face appears uninviting. I lack the soft lines associated with sensuality. I do look weird. But Willy didn't see me that way. When he broke up with me, he scoffed not at the evidence our friends laid out but their interpretation of it. He said he appreciated my solemnity and introverted disposition. He touched my bolt-like wrist bones and called me smart, empathetic, beautiful. The qualities that made me an easy target for other people's derision also made me interesting. To Willy, I wasn't the ugly duckling or the oddity. He singled me out as special. Alluring. He swore he was still attracted to me. It was just the timing. He needed to find his direction in life. He had things to figure out. Again and again, he placed the blame for our breakup on himself and not on me. I listened, bewildered. It didn't make sense. I couldn't understand why, if he liked me so much, he didn't want to date me anymore. That Willy paused to emphasize how much and in what ways I mattered to him infuriated me at seventeen, but it humbles me at thirty. He described me to myself, highlighting traits I hadn't thought anyone else valued or even cared enough to notice. I doubt either of us knew what he was doing, and if I heard that speech today, I'm sure it would sound pretentious and embarrassing and a little bit dumb.

But there's still something sweet about the way Willy anticipated my insecurities. It's sad, how I didn't see him trying to smooth over the cracks he knew he was creating. I think he wanted to instill in me the confidence I'd need to nurture the things he found remarkable about me despite what he knew I'd read as a rejection of everything secret I'd let him see.

5. On the ride to his place, David told me all about his heroin addiction. "But I'm not on that shit anymore," he said. "I'm on methadone now. I'll probably be off in, like, six months." I didn't know enough to understand the improbability of his timeline. I didn't even know what methadone was. "It's like synthetic heroin," David told me, though I'd known better than to ask. He spread out in my passenger seat and toyed with a pack of Marlboro Reds. David kept them in his T-shirt's front pocket like a 1950s rebel. "Can I smoke in here?" he asked. "Yeah. Just roll the window down," I said. I'd never let anyone smoke in my car, but I spoke as though it happened all the time. Between drags, David explained that he'd started doing drugs after he had his wisdom teeth removed. "I just sat around taking these pills and playing Nintendo," he said. "It was fun. I was, like, sixteen. I started getting Percocets and oxys and whatever. When I moved to New York, I got on heroin." Even now, David claims that he was in New York to attend NYU. But when the mom found out about his drug use, she had my aunt, a lawyer in Orlando, call the school. My aunt pretended she wanted to hire David and needed to check his references. NYU said it had no record of his enrollment. David explained away the discrepancy—he'd dropped out before the first semester ended, he said—but I couldn't entirely trust what he told me anymore. No matter how much I wanted to believe him or how deeply I buried my doubts, the phone call sowed a seed. On that first day, though, I trusted David completely. I didn't know any better. He told me he'd been doing well in college, even

cited a favorite English teacher. But then his girlfriend died, he said, and he left the city. I said the things you say: "I'm so sorry" and "I can't imagine." I was a teenager from a sheltered household in a small town. Of course I felt sympathy. Of course I believed in second chances. Of course I was susceptible to someone four years older who knew how to make a girl like me feel special. David had dealt in girls like me his entire life. Girls like the girl I was then are all over the Florida Panhandle. Populous as the fish the dad and I used to catch in the Choctawhatchee Bay. We are girls who swim hesitantly toward sin, shifting shape in the same easy way a rainbow trout's scales change color in the sun. David's hook slipped right under my skin, and I only noticed because it felt so good nestled in that empty space.

6. Willy's breakup talk was generous, and it was self-serving. Over the summer, Taylor told me that Willy actually broke up with me because he'd cheated. *Cheating* meant that Willy had made out with another girl because making out was all we'd ever done together. I never let him touch me between my legs. He'd slide his hand inside my panties, and I'd laugh and say, "Not that. Not yet. I can't." I wasn't sure what exactly Willy intended to do in there. Touch me, of course, but *touch* seemed an inadequate word to describe what it would mean to let someone mine my insides like that. I'd heard other girls talk about "getting fingered," and it sounded crass, ugly, almost violent. Whatever Willy wanted to do inside my underwear, I knew it would change me. It would hurt. It was sexual, and I wasn't supposed to want it. I definitely wasn't supposed to do it. Where, in other teenagers, mystery and prohibition arouse a charged curiosity, I felt only fear. In my head, sex most closely resembled stripping naked and asking someone to stab me. My inexperience was embarrassing, but I wanted to keep it. For Willy, I think that innocence enhanced the attraction. We'd both sworn to God that we wouldn't have sex outside of marriage, and he apparently

found abstinence more difficult a practice than I did. He liked testing his own boundaries as much as he liked testing mine. His van's front end was so wide Willy couldn't reach me from the driver's seat, so we'd sit in the cavernous back, and I'd pretend to consider letting him touch me in ways to which I never actually planned to consent. When Willy drove my car, he'd reach into the passenger seat, unbutton my jeans, and gnarl up his hand like the mom used to do when she sang "The Itsy Bitsy Spider" to my sisters and me. Willy would squeeze this ticklish spot a few inches above my knee, and each time I squealed more loudly because I did and didn't know what he was about to do. I always laughed—it was a reflex, but I also liked knowing I couldn't control my reaction, like whatever happened next was out of my hands—and I always tensed up, and then, for a few seconds, I'd actually relax. I'd open my legs, and Willy would creep his fingers up my thigh, pausing to rub his hand over the crotch of my jeans. Sometimes I let him peel back my underwear and touch the soft skin beneath it. I could stay still until his index finger angled upward, and then I'd sit up so straight my pelvic floor hit the coils beneath my Intrepid's cloth passenger seat. There wasn't room in my pants for his hand anymore. I recited my line: "Not yet. Not that. I can't." I wasn't teasing. I didn't intend to be mean. When Willy lifted his hand off or out of my jeans, my whole pelvis ached. But I knew if I let Willy touch me the way he wanted to touch me, no one would touch me the way Willy did ever again. Willy touched me like a porcelain doll he didn't want to break but knew he could if he changed his mind. He liked my hipbones, the way they protruded like handles, and I liked the way they looked exposed to someone else's eye. Sometimes he'd dig his thumbs into my thighs or abdomen or lower back until I bruised, or he bit down on my finger, my stomach, my clavicle. His shark-sharp teeth left red marks on me for hours or days. Once, he bit my neck between classes, and I returned to the picnic table with tiny rust-colored pinpricks on my pale skin.

I knew I was supposed to feel embarrassed or ashamed, but my indented flesh flushed with pride. When Taylor noticed, I said, "What? No. It's nothing," and pressed my palm to the place Willy's incisors had been; I wanted to feel that sting again. Like boys pulling girls' ponytails on playgrounds, bites and bruises were integral to the way Willy expressed and I accepted affection. Maybe it was possessive, his need to put our intimacy on display. But aside from the clumsy, half-oblivious way I lunged my pelvis at Willy's in private, we didn't have another way to mime sex. And he wasn't trying to hurt me. It didn't hurt, and I liked looking down at the sickly blue-brown circles and red notches with which he branded my body. Each one served as evidence that Willy wanted me, how much, and in what way.

7. David had me stop at the Wendy's off Highway 98 in Destin. He ordered a chocolate milkshake. He jammed a straw into the top of his cup. "Methadone gives you a sweet tooth," he said. I remember exactly the way he said it, the words a smug grin. He said it like his addiction gave him a leg up on the rest of the world, which he observed at a few steps' remove. We weren't far from his dad's auto shop. David lived there in a semi-converted attic apartment. To get inside, we had to climb the steepest flight of stairs I'd ever seen. They were almost vertical. David held my hand from two steps above, our bodies knocking against each other in the cramped space. "How long has it been since"—I fumbled for the right words—"since you came back?" My voice echoed off the bare walls. I couldn't bring myself to use her name (Jocelyn) or to say the words: *death*, *died*, *dead*. David turned around and shrugged like it was nothing. "A couple months," he said. He unlocked his door and ushered me in. "Wow," I said. "That's… I'm sorry." I couldn't finish. I didn't want to suggest to this person with whom I already wanted a future that maybe it was too soon for him to date again. The attic was like a long railroad

apartment. Most of its beams stood exposed, the walls skeletal suggestions of actual rooms. I sat on an orange-plaid couch David had shoved against the floor-to-ceiling windows on the south wall. Looking out them gave me vertigo. The height reduced the highway and the Wendy's we'd just left to a Lego tableau. The trees that obscured my bank's parking lot shrunk to shrubs. All of Destin spread beneath me in miniature. The north-facing windows looked down on a two-lane back road and a yellow sign that read *Tires Plus*, but all the windows were at least partially boarded up with plywood. When the shop was closed, David and I would often climb out on the roof to smoke cigarettes, but that afternoon Tires Plus was still open, and we stayed inside. David picked Interpol's *Turn on the Bright Lights* from atop a stack of records and dropped his turntable's needle into its grooves. He talked about this new band—"They're kind of a Joy Division rip-off, but they're pretty good," he said—while he dug around in a drawer for a film canister. He reached up and lifted a cheap plastic bong off a shelf. David thought it was funny that I'd never smoked pot. He didn't doubt my desire to do it, though I hadn't had any until he assumed I did. He packed the bowl, sat beside me on the couch, and showed me how to hit a bong. I fucked it up somehow. Pulled out the carb too soon or not at all. I didn't get stoned. David said a lot of people didn't get stoned on their first tries; it was okay. I don't remember how we started making out, but when we did, it was like I'd done it a thousand times with a thousand different men. I let go of all the inhibitions that had kept me so chaste with Willy. I felt mature, legs spread over David's lap and my hands in his hair. He didn't try to take off my shirt or unbutton my pants. He laid me out on my back, held up the edge of my T-shirt like a tent, and ran his hands across my belly. His fingertips traced each of my ribs and reached to thumb at my bra's underwire. I didn't need the wire. I was too flat-chested even for an A cup. I worried David would think I'd tricked him; the bra's thick synthetic fabric and poor fit made my breasts look bigger than they really were. But he didn't comment on their small size or my childlike figure. David had an adult's body: marble chest like a Renaissance statue's, a skull-and-crossbones tattooed on his right wrist, this strength in his arms that made me feel small and vulnerable, which I was. I could spread my whole body over David's with room to spare like in a baby picture where I'm curled on the dad's chest and he doesn't even need his hands to hold me in place. I don't remember why or how David and I stopped kissing, only the way I folded myself into his chest and dozed off with his chin against my scalp, the taste of cigarettes and processed chocolate on my tongue.

8. I ran into Willy at a party over the spring or summer or maybe winter break after David and I broke up. I was still young enough that I couldn't legally drink but old enough to know I should act jaded in front of the first person who broke my heart. I was sitting on the ground inside my friend's screened porch, alone but for my beer and a cigarette. Willy and I left the backyard and ambled over to the sidewalk to talk. "I'm sorry," Willy said. I gave him a confused side eye. "For what?" I asked. He told me he felt guilty about how he'd treated me in high school. "I think if I'd been better to you," he said, "you'd never have dated that guy in the first place." He meant David. "Thanks, I guess," I said. "But I probably would have dated David anyway." I didn't know how to react to a man's sincere apology. I was still young and angry and unable to see the ways relationships serve as templates for each other, how getting hurt in one might affect the next. But I knew I didn't like the power Willy attributed to his actions. His apology posited my interest in David as simply reactionary. It robbed me of agency and dismissed the electricity David sparked inside me. But what he said was also some kind of true. Otherwise, it wouldn't have bothered me; I might not remember it anymore. I turned my

back to him and eyed a streetlight. My skin raised goose pimples like scales on a lizard's tail; like cracked, stacked fingernails; like a snap in the twine that structured my spine. Willy had identified something powerless and frail in me that I didn't want to see. Something self-destructive and messy. I never got comfortable with Willy's hand up my shirt, yet David and I were all but fucking within the same four- or five-month period Willy spent as my boyfriend. The second time I hung out with David, I snorted cocaine and didn't hesitate. I doubt I did any of it consciously, but I'm sure I moved more quickly with David because I thought he'd dump me if I didn't. I could only have absorbed that belief from Willy. But I can't know what might have happened had Willy not broken up with me in the way he did, if he'd told me his real reason so the lack of one wouldn't have given my imagination such a big room to wander around in; I can't know what I'd have done with David if I'd never known that my first boyfriend was off with another girl while I agonized over how high up on my thigh I should let him put his hand. Maybe I wouldn't have dated the exact next person who expressed interest in me. Maybe I'd have listened to David's stories about death and abuse and decided I was unequipped or unwilling to write myself into such a collection. I might have seen how he manipulated me and had the confidence to walk away or at least assert my boundaries the way I had with Willy. But maybe those weren't really my boundaries. Maybe I kicked over the first barrier and decided I didn't need the others either. Maybe I needed David to show me that I liked trouble, or maybe I only thought I liked it. If I didn't look too closely, all the trouble David put me through looked a lot like love. When Taylor told me about the other girl, I drove to Willy's house and screamed at him. He listened and nodded, and when I cried, he put his arms around me and took on all my anger and all the blame. He admitted exactly what he'd done. He apologized. It was so easy. Maybe David confirmed my belief that love was hard; it was tumult and hurt, and someone who couldn't even yell back at me couldn't really have loved me in the first place. I don't know. But it's too easy to lay at someone else's feet all the ways I changed my shape.

9. I woke up on David's couch, the sky lit orange and glazed a deep hazy blue, split down the middle between sunset and sundown. I startled. I hadn't slept anywhere but my own bed since probably the sixth grade. And it was late, or later than I usually stayed out on school nights. "I have to go," I kept saying. "My parents don't know where I am. I never do this. What am I going to say?" David suggested I tell the truth. "You met someone. You lost track of time," he said. I couldn't explain to him that I was not the type of girl who came home at 9:00 p.m. on a Tuesday and told her parents she'd met a guy she liked. I made up something about being at Taylor's house. I almost remember pressing the giant digits on my car phone and calling Taylor to tell her that she and I had been together that afternoon and evening, and I almost remember telling her about David. But I don't know that I did. I simply told the mom the first of the hundred-thousand lies I'd tell so I could spend more time with David. I wasn't worried about getting caught. No one thought to question where I'd been or with whom I'd spent all those hours. I was a good kid, and no one knew yet that I'd stopped acting the part.

10. It took so little for me to change everything about myself. A bit of attention from an attractive guy, and I threw away years of order and spiritual cleanliness. I wasn't one of those kids who just never got the chance to do drugs. I could have done them. Almost everyone I knew had gone through a short drug phase in late-middle or early high school. Chelsea and Rebecca spent ninth grade smoking pot with guys they met in Grayton Beach, which used to serve more as a hippie outpost than the retreat for rich tourists that's

there now. When we were little, hardly anyone lived out on those beaches. We played house under trees with gnarled branches that bowed like rafters from their fat trunks. The limbs curled upward right where they should have met the ground so the trees hovered like enchanted floating caves. The leaves hid our tiny feet. By the time we were teenagers, condos and boutiques had encroached upon the forested beaches where we'd wandered in wonder on white-sand dunes. Chelsea and Rebecca went to parties thrown in the big new houses along the bayou. They got high in homes unlike ours, where adults didn't care that fifteen-year-olds got stoned in their bedrooms. Our parents didn't know what they were doing until the night Chelsea crashed her car into one of those majestic trees, grown up to the size of a redwood. In eighth grade, Taylor hung out with this older girl, Patricia, who took her to parties she didn't invite us to attend. I remember standing beside Taylor's teal locker at Destin Middle School while she told me about the first time she did cocaine. I thought she was disgusting. I thought Patricia was disgusting. I thought *Who would do that to themselves* as Taylor described the speedy thrill she got from rubbing coke on her gums. I thought Chelsea and Rebecca were stupid. I hated the way they acted when they got stoned, the condescending pleasure they took in being fucked up around people who weren't. I was never going to do drugs. Not ever. And then I did. I have no way to explain myself. I don't remember a switch lighting up in my brain or any secret curiosity; not once did I think any differently about drugs than I had before I took them: they were bad for your body and bad for your soul, and they could get you into trouble. But I couldn't say to a heroin addict that drugs were immoral or that I had no particular desire to try them. I couldn't admit that I'd been baptized in the D.A.R.E. logic cops preached at us in kindergarten classrooms or that the Bible said my body was a temple. To say all of that would have been cruel and judgmental and, really, untrue. When David passed me his bong, none of those reservations even crossed my mind. I only remember worrying that my parents would recognize the smell when I got home. But I didn't equivocate or hesitate. David offered, and I accepted. I guess I didn't want to be a good kid anymore; I didn't want worry and stress and fear to consume me. So I smoked pot. I didn't feel different or deviant or guilty, and that surprised me more than how easily I inhaled the smoke into my lungs.

11. On Wednesday nights, whoever wanted to come to youth group piled into our friend Zack's Denali, Beth's Jeep, Ahmed's Cutlass Supreme, or Daniel's beat-up maroon sedan, and we rode in a caravan to a nondenominational church near the Walton County line. Zack's grandfather served as pastor there. Our youth leader Jimmy, a man so large he sat in two metal folding chairs as if they were one, guided us in Bible study at the beginning of each meeting. One of us read a few verses, and we'd talk about what they meant and how they applied to our lives or belief systems. Around the time I met David, we were doing 1 Corinthians 11. Daniel stuttered through the eleventh chapter's first dozen or so verses. Jimmy watched me as if anticipating my objection. In 1 Corinthians 11:3, Paul asserts that *the head of every man is Christ, and the head of the woman is man, and the head of Christ is God.* Jimmy liked to chide me for my nascent feminism, as if resistance to patriarchy were a youthful affectation I'd renounce with time the way I had my year-long refusal to wear anything but dresses at the end of second grade. When I decided at fourteen that I didn't want children, Jimmy smirked and said I'd change my mind. He laughed when I wondered whether I even wanted to get married and why only I was expected to change my name if I did. He took my qualms with the Word of God more seriously. We debated biblical teachings that I found misogynist all the time, but only our argument over 1 Corinthians 11:1–10 sticks in my memory. I had never seen the passage before. A hum invaded

my head as I read silently ahead of Daniel. Jimmy started asking questions. I raised an eyebrow and leaned back in my chair. A couple of the boys made jokes. Ahmed said nothing; he only went to youth group because we did. Rebecca put her hand on my leg and said she was pretty sure 1 Corinthians had died with Jesus on the cross. Jimmy interpreted the offending words so I couldn't say that God treated women as second-class citizens. I don't remember exactly how he tried to allay my concerns, only that he didn't succeed. I simmered. We got stuck in all that talk of covered or uncovered and shaven versus shorn heads, the *ifs* and *thens*. And then I had to shut up because everyone else wanted to play basketball behind the fellowship hall. We'd spent the entire meeting discussing that verse, and I still didn't understand why women needed interlocution before God while men submitted only to Jesus. I didn't know when or why my creator had deemed me property, just that 1 Corinthians 11:8–9 stated in unambiguous, near-monosyllabic terms that I was: *the man is not of the woman; but the woman of the man*, Paul writes. *Neither was the man created for the woman; but the woman for the man.* My entire life, in Sunday school and at church-camp assemblies, people had said I was created in God's image. Yet 1 Corinthians 11:7 told me that *a man… is the image and glory of God*, but *the woman is the glory of the man*. According to the Methodists in whose church and faith I'd been baptized and confirmed, my Christian praxis glorified God. But in 1 Corinthians 11:7, I glorified the earthly man who headed me. My parents had lied when they said I could do anything a man could do, as had teachers who taught me to substitute *humankind* for *man* or *men* in ancient and prewar texts. Corinthians broke what faith I still had in God, in Jesus, in faith itself. No one was the head of me, and I refused to worship a deity who carved out special rules for His creations because some of us had vaginas. But my hurt and anger were based in more than principle now. I had felt, if only in miniature, the physical and psychic violence men could inflict on women. On me. If God intended that I submit to and accept as superior—if he'd granted additional power to—the sex with the greatest capacity to wound me, God had never loved me in the pure and unconditional way the mom and Zack's kindly old grandfather and even Jimmy had taught me He did. He could not love me if He put in charge of me the same people who, according to sex ed and Lifetime movies and Joyce Carol Oates and my own limited experience and the Bible itself, would cheat on and lie to and insult and rape and maim and murder me if granted the right opportunity. And, here, in 1 Corinthians 11:3–10, God granted men not only unlimited opportunity but the right. If God would have me submit to a man, I could not submit to God. I wasn't even sure I still believed in God. I kept going through the motions of belief, but I guess I'd always gone through the motions. I'd stood in auditoriums watching young Christians from all over the South sing updated, pseudo-rock hymns and wave their arms in praise. I never raised my arms. You raised your arms because the Holy Spirit moved you. When the Holy Spirit moved the kids around me, they looked like idiots.

12. David called the day after the day we met. The mom answered the phone and handed it to me with a kind of bemused ambivalence. I stood in the laundry room and laughed and said "Uh huh" and agreed to go to a movie on Friday. I told the mom instead of asking her, and she told me I could go. She could have said no or that she needed to meet David first, but she didn't; she trusted me. Of course I left things out. I didn't mention the drugs, and I said David was nineteen because I knew twenty-two was too old and that my parents wouldn't let me date a methadone patient. I hated lying to my parents, especially the mom, but it got me out of the house and into David's apartment. He met me outside the shop and led me up those tall, dark stairs to his room. His friend Nina lay stretched across his mattress like a big, skinny cat. Really,

Nina was David's best friend Gideon's little sister. She wasn't much older than I was—nineteen or twenty. But, in my memory, she's so assured and sophisticated that she could have been 30. Nina applied black eyeliner in flawless rings around her huge blue eyes, and she wore these black ballet flats like the ones I'd seen on French movie stars. She looked like Audrey Hepburn with red hair. Beside her, I felt unkempt and embryonic. If I saw Nina now, she'd probably look like any other nineteen-year-old girl: baby faced, awkward, her outfit an obvious costume. But back then I thought she looked like an actual adult. She knew what she was doing when she set out her own line of coke from her own little bag. I couldn't decide whether Nina posed a threat to me. She and David bickered and teased like siblings. I sat between them and stared at my hands; I was supposed to watch David, who held a straw to his nose and leaned over a slice of cocaine in the slow, instructive way a biology teacher might wield her scalpel before students who've yet to dissect frogs on their own. Nina watched me swallow my first methadone pill and snort the fat line David cut for me as if I were an exhibit in a freak show: The Little Clean Girl. She must have thought I was crazy, jumping straight to the hardest drugs without asking how they would make me feel or what they could do to me, in what ways I could get hurt. I had this fear that Nina was judging me, and I wasn't sure why it mattered except it made me wonder whether David was, too. I wasn't sure what David wanted with me when he could have had a girl whose drug use he didn't have to initiate. But maybe that was part of the fun. Maybe David, like Willy, found my inexperience endearing. Maybe he liked watching me turn into someone else right there beside him. Maybe he was as curious as I was.

13. At some point I must have realized that David wasn't actually trying to get clean. I don't remember feeling disappointed in him or reticent about falling for a drug addict. Methadone and cocaine and Xanax made me feel bright

and clear and sure of myself, and I guess I understood why David couldn't or wouldn't give that up. I wouldn't have wanted him to—not anymore. If David had quit using opiates, I'd have had to quit, too, right as I was getting started. I didn't want to stop. I wanted to go and go until I turned myself inside out and could see what I was like when anxiety and convention didn't govern my decisions. For eighteen years, I'd decided I could only be good, and when I let that dictate go, I grew out of and into myself. I let it go and did what David did because I wanted him to like me, but I also let it go because I could. David had never known the girl I'd been before—the good girl, the clean one—so I didn't need to uphold her image. Sometimes I wonder what kind of woman I'd be now if I'd never met David or if I'd insisted on remaining the same girl I'd always been when I did. I don't think I want to know that person. When I imagine her, she isn't any of the things I value in myself now. She's not brave or tough or confident. She doesn't assert herself or commit to anything that might end in failure. She's boring and predictable, unbroken. Sometimes I think if I'd cared less about whether David liked me and more about keeping myself intact, I'd have ended up too safe, too careful, too clean, too good.

14. Nina left after she procured another gram of coke for David and me with the cash I got at Walmart. We had to buy something, so David grabbed a fat Bic lighter and set it on the cashier's conveyor belt. I scrawled *fifty-two and 23/100* above the "pay to the order of" line on a check. I couldn't hold my hand steady. I knew the cashier knew exactly why I wanted that extra money; she could probably tell I was high, too. I kept my eyes on the dirtied white toes of my Converse, the brown-flecked eggshell of the linoleum floor. I don't know why it mattered if the cashier knew we'd exchange the money for cocaine or noticed my pinned pupils, but it did. I guess it made the change in me visible. I gave her a shy nod and followed David out the automatic doors. In the park-

ing lot, I handed Nina two twenties and a ten. She drove us back to Tires Plus and went across the street to buy the coke at Harbor Docks, the restaurant where she worked. She walked back into David's apartment and tossed him a small, clear bag half filled with white powder. "You're going to kill that girl," she said to him as she turned to go. To me she said, "Don't try and keep up with him. You don't know what you're doing." She was right; I didn't know a single thing about drugs. But David knew everything, and that made me feel safer than I was. When I was lying beside him inside that cozy methadone euphoria and bright, fast-forwarded cocaine high, nothing could hurt me.

15. When I was 20, my friend Tom said, "It's weird. You'll experiment with drugs without even thinking about it, but you don't experiment with sex." Tom was the first person who put his penis inside me. He hadn't done it yet—I was still too scared—but we'd talked about it. I think Tom thought my fear was cute. I think he liked knowing I'd decided to let him finally push it aside. We had sex right before Thanksgiving, and he didn't call me over the holiday break. I spent most of the week in Destin, and I didn't call him, either. I wanted to see how much time would pass before one of us broke. I ran into Tom downtown the next weekend, when I was back in Gainesville. I didn't say anything right away; I just acted cold. "What's wrong?" he asked. We were standing in front of the Speakeasy, a 1920s-themed bar where we went for cheap martinis on Wednesday nights. I said, "You knew that was my first time, and you didn't even call me after." Tom said he didn't think of what we'd done as actual sex. I still can't figure out what he did think or what he meant. What we'd done was definitely sex. Tom's dick had split me in two. I bled through his mattress, ruined it on both sides. But the blood heated my insides to silk, and after a few minutes, I forgot the pain. I wanted Tom's weight on me constantly and to stare forever at the determined, cautious look on his face

that told me I was safe, that he didn't want to hurt me. That Tom didn't want to hurt me obviously meant he cared about me, and I needed the first person who put his dick inside me to care about me in the uncomplicated, absolute way I didn't think David ever had. "There's no way you can call that anything but sex," I insisted. Tom said he was sorry. He should have called me. "But that's not what I call sex," he said. I felt like a fool. I'd been walking around all week thinking I'd had sex, and the person I thought I'd had it with was telling me it hadn't happened. "Then what was it?" I asked. "Something else," Tom said. Months later, Tom and I fucked like dogs in my twin-sized bed. We finished, and he said, "See, *that's* sex." I didn't know what else to think but that Tom defined sex by whether or not it was fun for him and that the slow, deliberate way he'd fucked me the first time hadn't been. When I tried to articulate the difference between drugs and sex, I said, "Drugs can't hurt my feelings. It's different. Your emotions don't get involved." Tom disagreed. "Fucking with your emotions is sort of what drugs do," he said. I shrugged. "It's different." A drug, I was trying to explain, couldn't fuck me and tell me later that, actually, it hadn't because it didn't enjoy the experience. The ache Tom's denial burned into my ribcage still hadn't healed. I'm not sure it ever will. That Tom hadn't liked my blood and inert body and his role in removing a piece of the skin I'd worked so hard to shed over the past two years hurt so much, I think, because I'd loved every stinging second of it.

16. David tells me that the impression I have of myself at eighteen is not at all what he remembers. *I never really imagined you as a vulnerable young kid in high school*, he wrote in a text message twelve years later. David has also said he had no personality then, that he was just a bunch of chemicals firing from neuron to neuron, a body stalking its next fix. But the David I remember is as charismatic and cruel as anyone I've known. I thought sometimes that his

personality was too big and too boisterous, and I wished he'd turn it down a notch. Neither of us remembers the other in the right way. I'm sure I was not as vulnerable as I feel when I remember these things and that David was neither as charming as I thought him nor as inanimate as he thinks himself. I was naïve, but I guess I couldn't have been innocent. I wanted Parking Lot Guy from the second I saw him. But I didn't *want* him—not sexually, not really; I wanted my idea of a relationship with him. I didn't know what I was getting into. I didn't know I could have what I wanted or what it meant to want in that way. I was a kid. Except that David doesn't think so. *I never imagined you as a vulnerable young kid…* And he probably didn't. I think I forget sometimes that David was only 22. Four years means more when you're eighteen than it does when you're 30. He was at least as vulnerable as I was, if not more so—a fact I like to forget so I can cast myself as the victim. But back then, to me, David really did seem so much older. He lived in his own little dwelling. He had an entire history, an actual backstory, that I felt I lacked. I built a new story, slowly, with David by my side. And maybe that's the me he remembers: the later me, the me I became with him. Perhaps he's confused that girl in the mall with the one who could hang with coke dealers and not blink because she knew she wasn't supposed to blink. Or maybe he really didn't think of me the way I did. Why would he? He didn't know who I was before I met him, and he didn't know what our relationship did to me until I told him when we were both in our 30s. Here, I'm remembering the best parts of David, the parts that drew me to him. There are other memories. And memory is faulty. Memory fractures and morphs; it solidifies like poured concrete. I break mine into pieces and look at each one, turn them over in my hand and let them slice my skin. If I let the blood run until the cuts scab over, I can pick at the dried wounds and start again. Not everyone remembers that way. Most people cover their scars, let the scab fall off on its own, avert their eyes when the needle goes in.

A GLOSSARY OF TERMS: EXCERPTS FROM *AN ENCYCLOPEDIA OF IATROGENIC OPIATE ADDICTION*

Butalbital with Codeine (*noun*): **1.** Compound used to treat acute pain, particularly migraine pain. Consists of the barbiturate butalbital (50 milligrams) and the opiate pain reliever codeine (30–40 mg) mixed with caffeine (40 mg) and acetaminophen or aspirin (325 mg). Better known by its brand names, Fioricet and Fiorinal. Nomenclature depends on which non-narcotic analgesic the pill contains. Fioricet in particular may cause medication-overuse headaches and rebound migraines brought on by patients' physical dependence on acetaminophen. Both combination products carry said risk, however, as headaches are a primary symptom of caffeine withdrawal and an uncommon but still possible side effect of butalbital itself. Barbiturate withdrawal can be fatal, and patients should not discontinue use unless under a doctor's supervision. **2.** Butalbital with codeine works on your chronic daily headaches like a fountain drink works on a hangover. You can actually, physically feel it fizzing away the pain. No other drug fully relieves a headache the way butalbital with codeine does; it even banishes settled migraines. You don't habituate to it quickly, so you can take a dozen or so pills every day for at least a year and still obtain relief, even get high. Your California doctor neglects to mention the rebound migraines. He doesn't tell you barbiturate withdrawal can kill you. He refills and refills and refills your butalbital with codeine. He'll write you something like six refills before you leave California for a new job in D.C. You won't need a doctor during your two-month stint in the nation's capital, which is lucky since you get laid off or maybe fired—you're still not sure which—before you're eligible for company insurance or even unemployment. You move back to your mother's house in Florida and see Dr. Hert, his name doubly ironic given the man's reputation as an easy target for addicts seeking recreational painkillers. Dr. Hert says he's never heard of butalbital with codeine. He tries to replicate it with **Vicodin** and butalbital, but separating the chemicals flattens their soda-fizz sizzle. You'll drop the barbiturate and rely on the Vicodin. You won't take butalbital with codeine again until you wake up with a migraine the morning you and your mother have to drive thirteen hours to the Virginia college town that houses your graduate creative writing program. You've spent the year off opiates (*see also*: **Suboxone** *and* **Withdrawal**), and every pained nerve in your body itches for narcotic relief. You'll visit three urgent care centers before you land an actual appointment with an actual doctor at an actual medical clinic, the Sacred Heart satellite office in Miramar Beach. This doctor offers you **Compazine**. In the seven years you've spent Googling cures and experimenting with migraine medications, no doctor or internet article, no fellow migraineur or well-meaning armchair physician has ever mentioned Compazine. The Sacred Heart doctor says Compazine "might" dull the scalpel-sharp ache that runs from your nose to the tip at the top of your spine. "This migraine could last a week. I'm driving all day with my mom," you tell him. "'Might' won't cut it." The doctor sits back in his chair and asks as though offering you a cup of coffee, "How about some Fiorinal?" You nod. "Perfect," you say as you shake the doctor's hand and reach for the prescription. "I'll only take it if the Compazine doesn't work," you promise your mom as she drives to CVS. Two hours later, she's pulling into a rest stop so you can vomit Compazine-pink bile onto steaming Alabama concrete instead of inside her new car. You take the Fiorinal. On Fiorinal, you are clear and focused. You are motivated. You hang all your clothes in your closet and two new paintings on your walls. While your mom sleeps at her hotel, you write. You write until dawn. In the morning, your mom bangs and bangs on your door, sure you're dead because you don't open it or answer your phone. Later, when you get back on **Oxycodone**, she will remind you over and over of this morning when you took narcotics and didn't wake up. The story reinforces her worst fears about your painkillers. But Fiorinal reminds you what it's like to have a head that doesn't always hurt. Faced with the instant relief Fiorinal provides, the year and a half you spent getting and staying "clean" (*see also*: **Suboxone**, **Withdrawal**, *and* **Post-Acute Withdrawal Syndrome**) feels wasted and ridiculous. Your mother will always in part blame your return to oxycodone on the doctor who took your history and wrote you an opiate anyway. When she speaks of oxycodone, she speaks in the language of recovery and hope, as though trading the pain in your head and all of your bodily autonomy for the stigmatic pricks and the obsessive logistics and the animal fear that accompany opioid dependence constitutes relapse. But going back isn't relapse; it's resignation, a confirmation of your need.

Clonidine (*noun*): **1.** Antihypertensive drug. Also prescribed for Attention Deficit Hyperactivity Disorder; off-label to relieve anxiety, diarrhea, and menopausal hot flashes; and for chronic migraine and headache disorders. Eases discomfort associated with cessation of opiate, alcohol, and nicotine use in the physiologically dependent. **2.** Paul, your doctor in New York, says your headaches are probably vascular. He suggests you try blood pressure pills. Neither of you is ready for **Topamax**, the neurologists' go-to with which most migraineurs would begin; you've read about its side effects and agree with Paul's contention that it's best to start with lower-stakes curatives. The hypertension meds he initially writes you promise side effects so comparatively mild they might as well not exist. You'll take **Propranolol** and **Verapamil** for a few weeks each and feel nothing. Maybe a little fatigue, but your headaches don't change. You won't understand why Paul calls clonidine "the blood pressure medicine of last resort" until the morning after the night you forget to take your evening pill. You wake up with a head made of glass. Someone is trying to pry it open with an icepick. You call Paul. He says your blood pressure is too high. You need to keep down a clonidine for one full hour—any less time and you won't know for sure that your body digested it. The glass head spews vomit, ejecting each pill you feed it, until you fall asleep in the early afternoon. You wake up to skin and bone hardened around the icepick, which remains in place for 24 hours. You program a reminder into your phone so you can't forget your clonidine again. If you doubt at all that you took it, you swallow a backup. You'll know if you doubled your dose because an extra clonidine puts you right to sleep. Clonidine reduces the frequency and severity of your migraines, or so you'll think; you can never really tell, but you won't quit taking it. You believe too much in its power and doubt you can handle even tapering off. Anyway, clonidine is easy. Clonidine is so easy you sometimes forget to refill it until you're staring into your bottle at a single pill. Even after you leave New York and stop paying to be his patient, you can email Paul, and he'll call you in a year's worth of refills. Of your three major medications, only clonidine doesn't feel like a constant emergency.

Combination Product (*noun*): **1.** Term used to refer to a class of narcotic drugs containing a secondary analgesic, usually acetaminophen or ibuprofen. Examples include Vicodin (hydrocodone and acetaminophen), Percocet (oxycodone and acetaminophen), Fiorinal/Fioricet (codeine, the barbiturate butalbital, and either acetaminophen or aspirin), and Vicoprofen (hydrocodone and ibuprofen). In 2014, the US Food and Drug Administration (FDA) limited the amount of acetaminophen allowed in combination products to 325 milligrams per pill; until that point, Vicodin contained 500 mg. Vicoprofen, the most common ibuprofen combination product, contains 200 mg. Doctors, pharmaceutical companies, and regulatory agencies believe that adding acetaminophen and NSAIDs to narcotic painkillers deters abuse, but such drugs pose serious risks of their own. Acetaminophen, especially if used in the management of chronic pain, may damage patients' livers, and ibuprofen combinations cause damage to the stomach and kidneys and render patients vulnerable to bleeding gastric ulcers. Moreover, medical literature sets hydrocodone's known lethal dose at 90 mg, while acetaminophen overdose initiates at 4,000 mg. Until the FDA rule change in 2014, a pain patient or recreational user needed only to take four 10 mg Vicodin pills to overdose not on the hydrocodone but the acetaminophen paired with it. Though preferred by some physicians and chronic pain patients, doctors generally limit their prescriptions of combination products to short-term patients such as those with post-operative pain. Long-term opioid therapy is usually conducted with "pure" opioids: a synthetic opiate sans NSAIDs and other additives. **2.** Because no one considers your headaches serious or actually chronic, doctors at first write you combination products: **Butalbital with Codeine**, **Vicodin**, **Vicoprofen**. When Dr. Hert switches you off the Fiorinal, you'll ask him for Vicoprofen in an ex-post-facto attempt to protect your liver, preferring instead to endanger your stomach. In New York, you'll coax Vicoprofen from doctors at the Beth Israel walk-in clinic and at Brooklyn Preferred Health Partners, the only medical offices that take your insurance and employ doctors willing to write your drug of choice. You don't move to pure opioids until a BPHP doctor tells you that his practice won't write "this stuff" for you again. You have to find a steady doctor. You find Paul via Google. He doesn't look promising. He's young—in his 40s—which means he went to medical school not long before dire warnings about drug seekers and addiction replaced the pain-management maxims "Believe the patient" and "Treat the pain first." In his description of himself, Paul comes off as optimistic and upbeat. Young, optimistic, upbeat doctors don't usually prescribe narcotics. They rave about meditation and extol the virtues of exercise before writing prescriptions for Topamax and Tylenol 3. But when you meet Paul, your worry diminishes. He looks like Anderson Cooper minus the silver hair: soft eyes, slightly oversized forehead, high cheekbones. He scrunches his brows and cocks his head while he listens to you talk the way the CNN anchor does when listening to interview guests. You tell Paul the story you've memorized by now: that first week-long migraine in 2008, how it returned once a month and then every second week, the way it multiplied and metastasized until you had—you have—a headache every day. You describe the headaches as precisely as you can. "But they're always different," you say, touching your head to indicate the places that bear the bulk of the pain. You answer Paul's questions, which cover both the physical and the psychological effects of your condition. You tell him how your pain exhausts you: it keeps you up and wakes you up and weighs you down; it never stops, and you never stop thinking about it. You admit to Paul that you're afraid your friends will stop inviting you to do things because you almost never accept anymore. You don't say you're scared you don't leave your apartment enough, but you think he intuits it. You list the medications you've taken to combat the headaches: **Midrin** and a couple of **Triptans**, Fiorinal, Vicodin, Vicoprofen. Paul asks how well the **Hydrocodone** works for you. "Okay, I guess," you say. New-patient appointments are essentially interviews. The doctor evaluates your fitness for the established patient role while you attempt both to discern whether the doctor's praxis aligns with your needs and to present yourself as a problem the doctor wants to solve. You perform your pain, perform legitimacy, perform fragility, perform your need and desperation so you read as equally responsible and pitiful. You're not performing in the sense of fakery; your performance is more like a megaphone, like turning up the volume so loud that your pain makes waves in the air, builds its own echo chamber. You perform because you know doctors think you're performing, because you watched your ex-boyfriend fake a herniated disc so that doctors would write him exactly what you hope Paul will write you. You perform because you are young and look anorexic, and there's nothing visibly wrong with your head. You perform so Paul will see how much you hurt and because you are never asking for simple continuation. Your current regimen is a starting point. It's fine. It works. But there's no such thing as too much pain relief. You play the part of Someone Who Needs More. With Paul, your performance elicits the review you hoped it would. "From what you've told me," he says, "I don't think the hydrocodone is controlling your pain. You haven't taken Percocet?" he asks. You shake your head even though of course you've taken Percocet. It's not a lie because you've never taken Percocet for your headaches. "I'd like to try oxycodone, then," Paul says. You startle at the suggestion of a stronger drug. You're okay with moving up to oxycodone, you say, but you hesitate. "It's just that I'm worried about my liver." And that's not a lie either. You really do worry about your liver. You tell Paul about the headaches you had as a kid, which you forgot to mention when he took your history. You hadn't connected your adult headaches to those of your childhood until Paul asked you his intake questions. Talking about acetaminophen evokes the bitter, blunt taste of the Tylenol your mom crushed and fed you in big spoonfuls until you were old enough to swallow pills on your own. Paul draws the blood with which he'll check your liver enzymes and hormone levels to ensure that the 20-plus years you've spent overtaking over-the-counter pain meds haven't damaged the organ and because the mom is convinced that your headaches stem from some hormonal imbalance, and you told her you'd have them tested. As you watch your blood fill his syringe, Paul asks how you think the acetaminophen and ibuprofen added to your narcotics affect your pain (*see also*: **Combination Product** *and* **Prednisone**). You say they don't really—but how would you know? You know only that you don't want Tylenol and ibuprofen contaminating your drugs if you have a choice. "Well, if the Tylenol's not doing much, why don't we just do plain oxycodone?" Paul says. You pretend again to hesitate, shrug, say, "Okay." Paul leans over his prescription pad. You relax into your shitty folding chair, the kind with a thin cushion on its seat and back. You've found your doctor. You take his prescriptions—Paul also writes your Klonopin and a prescription for the beta blocker **Propranolol**—to the Rite Aid near the group practice where you'll only see him once or twice. He opens his own office on East 4th Street between Broadway and Lafayette before the end of the year. Ditching hydrocodone and ibuprofen (*see also*: **Vicodin**) turns you into a serious pain patient. Pharmacists can no longer mistake you for someone who just had her wisdom teeth pulled. They know when you hand over your prescription that you mean to take these pills, to obtain them at this pharmacy, for the foreseeable future. Paul ups your dose and ups your dose and ups your dose at your request. And that makes you less a pain patient than a pain in everyone else's DEA-fearing asses.

Elavil (*proper noun*): **1.** Brand name of the tricyclic antidepressant amitriptyline. Initially used to treat depression and anxiety disorders, including Attention Deficit Hyperactivity Disorder and bipolar disorder, but since the development of selective serotonin reuptake inhibitors (SSRIs), amitriptyline is rarely a first-line depression treatment. The drug is more often prescribed off-label to treat migraines, neuropathic pain disorders such as fibromyalgia, and irritable bowel syndrome. Side effects include pounding or fluttering heartbeat; confusion or hallucinations; seizure or restless muscles; numbness, burning pain, or tingly feeling; constipation or urinary retention; drowsiness or dizziness; loss of appetite; dry mouth or unpleasant taste; trouble concentrating; blurred vision; decreased sex drive; and headache. Approved by the FDA in 1961. **2.** You first try amitriptyline in New York. Paul says, "It might help you relax, too," and hands you a prescription. You fold it over the ones for **Klonopin** and **Oxycodone** and hand the baby-blue bundle to the Duane Reade pharmacist, cocky like *See, I really do have headaches*, defensive like *Look, I'm really trying here*. But you only take one pill one time. You take it at night and hear a deep voice instructing you in a language you don't recognize from a vaguely familiar place deep inside your body. The place is dark, dank, cave-like. You can see it when you close your eyes. The voice flickers like static, its echo drifting from one clammy wall to another. It emanates from a man's disembodied head that looks like the Wizard's in *The Wizard of Oz* backlit in blue and black instead of green. The voice wants to tell you something important, but you don't know what it's saying, and now you're sinking into your mattress, your body like an elevator going down slow and smooth. You call Paul in a panic. He gets why you don't want to take amitriptyline again, but you're both disappointed. Now that you've dispensed with amitriptyline, you've only got the scary brain medications left to try: **Topamax, DHE, Neurontin**. Three years later, over the summer after your first year in your MFA program, you ask Paul for a new amitriptyline prescription. You can't get in to see a pain specialist until August, the student health center won't work on chronic medical issues, and you've spent the last year denying that you have a chronic medical issue, so you don't have a local primary care physician who could prescribe amitriptyline for you. "I'm thinking it might not make me feel crazy now that I'm off the oxycodone," you tell Paul. He says he's sorry to hear that you're getting headaches again. You don't tell him you never stopped or that, if the amitriptyline doesn't help, you're giving yourself permission to get back on oxys when whatever the Blacksburg Center for Pain Management suggests doesn't work either. You fill the prescription in April but wait until you're at your mom's new house in Florida to take it; if you descend into your mattress or see the cave or hear the voice again, you don't want to be in your house alone. You don't hear the voice or see the cave or feel like you're being lowered into a grave when you take your second first amitriptyline pill in late May. You don't really feel anything. By the time you do, around mid June, it's hard to tell what's your body's normal state and what's the drug fucking with your norepinephrine and serotonin. Your moods swing less often and with less intensity, easy and slow as a rocking-chair runner, but your pain is unmoved. In early July, a buzzy, electrical ache encircles your head and settles there like a shock collar inserted between your skull and skin. At first you think it's your period or the weather or stress or what you're eating. But nothing you do diminishes the charge. About ten weeks after your second first amitriptyline pill, you email Paul to tell him you've decided again to quit taking the drug. It doesn't work, and it mimics in miniature the way you felt on **Prozac**: stuck in an emotional purgatory, unable to rise above or fall below a mid-level contentment. The current that tickled your head dissipates within days. You're angry at the pills for exacerbating the pain they were supposed to relieve and at yourself for feeling disappointed. You knew better than to hope, but you guess you hoped anyway.

Klonopin (*proper noun*): **1.** Brand name for the generic drug clonazepam. Used primarily to prevent seizures and treat anxiety disorders, including social phobia and panic disorder, as well as childhood epilepsy; restless leg syndrome, bruxism, and other muscle problems; acute mania and psychosis; and some forms of parasomnia. Like other benzodiazepine formulations such as Xanax, Valium, and Ativan, Klonopin attaches itself to the same brain receptors as does alcohol. Habit-forming if taken for long periods and thus not recommended for the treatment of generalized anxiety disorder, though many patients take Klonopin for that purpose. Side effects include sedation; memory loss; suicidal ideation; muscle weakness; dry mouth; confusion; hallucinations; painful, difficult, or more frequent urination; unusual or involuntary eye movements; loss of appetite; nausea, diarrhea, or constipation; insomnia; respiratory depression; pale skin and easy bruising or bleeding; liver problems; and headache. Drinking alcohol increases most side effects. Withdrawal can induce or increase seizures, which may prove fatal. Taken by mouth in pill or wafer form. Initially patented in 1964 and brought to the US market in 1975. **2.** In your first semester as a women's studies grad student, you drink three big glasses of red wine at your advisor's Thanksgiving dinner and arrive home right in time for *Grey's Anatomy*, which you watch supine on your couch every Thursday night with a pipe full of ground-up weed in your right hand. In *Grey's Anatomy's* 2006 Thanksgiving episode, surgical intern Christina Yang runs from the operating room covered in blood, no longer able or willing to help her boyfriend, attending cardiac surgeon Preston Burke, hide the hand tremor he developed following neurosurgery performed by tentpole-character Meredith Grey's on-again-off-again lover Derek Shepherd. The episode is intense, its cuts quick and furious. You think your heart is pounding because you're so involved in this story you've watched since its 2005 debut on ABC. Then you think your heart is pounding because you need a cigarette, which doesn't make sense, but you're thinking about the things on which your body relies that aren't the water you've been drinking to stave off a hangover or the food you ate earlier, which all tasted of the same homey spice you love but can't place. You'll go outside to smoke and throw your American Spirit into your neighbors' yard when nicotine only quickens your pulse. You're going to die. Your heart can't keep beating this hard. The only explanations your heart could possibly offer for beating this hard point to your death. Your left arm tingles and throbs. Maybe you're having a heart attack. But isn't your right arm the heart-attack arm? You don't know. You're dying. It doesn't matter how or why. You pace your living room, debate going to the emergency room. It's Thanksgiving. You'll wait for hours as fathers stagger in with carving knives stabbed into their hands and drunken undergraduates drag friends through the automatic doors to have their stomachs pumped. You drive yourself to the ER anyway. It's right there; you can see it out your window if you crane your neck. If you die, what difference will it make if you do it in your house or a hospital waiting room? At least if you die in the ER, someone will call your mom. You try to explain what's happening to a nurse, but you can barely speak. Since you might, the nurse tells you, be having a heart attack, you don't have to wait. You're rushed into a bed and hooked up to an EKG monitor. But you aren't having a heart attack. "It's just a panic attack," the doctor tells you. He writes you a dozen Xanax and sends you home. At home, you take two pills and feel weightless and sedated. You're calm enough to call the Gainesville After Hours Clinic the next day and make an appointment with Dr. Grant, who always wrote David whatever he wanted. At your appointment, you tell Grant you had a panic attack, and the ER doctor wrote you Xanax. "But I don't want to take Xanax forever," you say. It's more addictive. It doesn't last as long. You break doctor shopping's cardinal rule and just tell him what you want: Klonopin. He writes you a month's worth anyway. Sixty one-milligram pills. Take as needed. You take it every day. That you're making a decision with each pill does not occur to you. You don't really think about the consequences: dependence, addiction, what psychiatrists call "brain wasting." You're 22. What do you care about consequences?

Midrin (*proper noun*): **1.** Combination analgesic, sedative, and vasoconstricting stimulant medication used in the treatment of headaches. Composed of acetaminophen (analgesic), dichloralphenazone (sedative), and isometheptene (vasoconstrictor/stimulant). Taken at migraine onset, Midrin, also known as Amidrine, Duradrin, Epidrine, or Nodolor, aborts attacks in 70–80 percent of patients. Also used to treat non-migrainous vascular and tension-type headaches. The large quantity of acetaminophen in Midrin may damage the liver and lead to liver failure, particularly in patients with histories of alcohol abuse or genetic predispositions to liver problems. Overtaking Midrin causes medication overuse, or "rebound," headaches and may result in physical dependence on acetaminophen. **2.** You will confuse doctors and possibly yourself trying to name Midrin. Your California doctor calls it "Dichlor," to which you can find no reference online or in the instructions and warnings that accompany the quintetially titled drug. You don't expect Midrin to do anything. It's a giant Tylenol. But Midrin will abort your migraines sans side effects until it up and quits a few months in. Its efficacy will not slowly diminish; you'll take it one day and miss the creeping relief that usually accompanies your dose. "Oh, it does that," your doctor will say when you express concern, as if this were not something you'd have wanted to know before you started relying on the drug. He'll suggest no new abortive or preventive medication. He leaves you to addict yourself to **Butalbital with Codeine**, which you don't mind. You're convinced you'll have these headaches for the rest of your life, and you're prepared to hide them behind narcotic painkillers until you die. You'll arrive in New York an addict and not unwittingly. You knew what you were doing. But your California doctor didn't prepare you for the mound of treatment options available to you (*see also*: **Clonidine**, **Elavil**, **Topamax**, *and* **Triptans**) or the cabal of doctors pushing them like bogeyman heroin dealers in 1990s cartoons and public service announcements. Their sneering dismissals of your pain as strange and temperamental, a consequence of your overactive mind and too delicate female body, shock you only slightly more than the prevailing preference for treating you like a lab rat. Why won't these men in their white coats accept, as you have, that your head hurts all the time, that nothing they can do will stop it, that only as an addict can you live the full life they say these other drugs will offer you?

Oxycodone (*noun, generic drug name*): **1.** Narcotic analgesic used in the treatment of moderate to severe pain. Side effects include mild confusion, respiratory depression, dizziness, drowsiness, fainting, stomach pain, nausea, constipation, itching skin, hyperalgesia—increased pain due to increased pain-receptor sensitivity—and risk of overdose. Notable brand names include Oxycontin, the spectacle around which ignited an ongoing national debate about prescription drug abuse and led to tightened restrictions on opioid prescribing. **2.** Your sister Beth, an MD and OB/GYN, loves to remind you that the American Neurological Association (ANA) dissuades doctors from prescribing opioids such as **o**xycodone for headache relief. You read the same memo for a research paper you wrote on your own condition. "They call it 'appropriate in some cases.' Maybe I'm one of those cases," you argue, but Beth says that's statistically unlikely. Do you think you're special or something? She implores you to "just try" the prescription NSAIDs and migraine prophylactics the ANA does recommend for conditions like yours. The ANA doesn't recommend anything for exactly your condition. The ANA hasn't even named your condition, not exactly. Still, Beth wants you to see how you tolerate **Celebrex** and **Neurontin**. You list the side effects you've heard on TV commercials: body aches and pains, muscle aches and pains, chest pain, jaw pain, eye pain, sunken eyes, blindness, severe stomach pain, stomach bleeding, non-menstrual vaginal bleeding, diarrhea, constipation, kidney problems, agitation, depression, confusion, slurred speech, hallucinations, suicidal ideation, wrinkled skin, stiff neck, broken bones, fast or irregular heartbeat, heartburn, high blood pressure, no blood pressure, no pulse, unexplained weight gain, loss of appetite, loss of voice, loss of consciousness, headache. "Headache!" you say to Beth. "But you won't get all the side effects," your doctor sister says even though she knows you've given up on drugs from **Elavil**

to **Zoloft** due to adverse reactions. Your body is sensitive; it is special. You don't like putting substances in it that bide their time so that, when you and your doctor assess their efficacy, you no longer know what's you as you know yourself and what's the pill imprinted after a month or three on the inside of your veins. With narcotics, you know why you're tired or itchy or constipated: you took a pill. Narcotics—and you get that this sounds counterintuitive—feel safe. But Beth's MD, her fear and hurt feelings, trump your experience, your preferences, your pain. Chelsea, your lawyer sister, loves to remind you that you chose opioids—twice—so you can't cry foul when she questions your motives for taking them or whine when people make assumptions about you based on the pill bottles in your purse pockets, even if those people share your DNA and your parents and your nose the way Beth and Chelsea do. "That's how life is," Chelsea says. She says it all the time, as if everyone's life revolves around the hoops you have to hurl your body through to prove you deserve a controlled substance to control your pain. Your psychiatrist at Virginia Tech loves to remind you that taking narcotics will make your life harder than a healthy person's, like you don't already know that. Like you could will yourself out of pain if only you'd stop taking oxys and **Klonopin** and smoking weed. You tell him you tried that. Post detox, when you couldn't depend on opioids anymore, you got dependent on Advil (*see also*: **Prednisone**). You limited yourself to three Advil per 48 hours and got stoned all day, which only sort of worked. Last semester, you couldn't find decent weed anywhere in Blacksburg, and you got a week-long migraine twice a month; your mother starts driving you back to Virginia after winter and summer breaks with vacuum-sealed ounces in your suitcase, and the number drops to about one every twelve weeks. Your mother does not love to but reminds you anyway that you were off oxys and didn't have to go back. Oxycodone reminds her that you hurt in ways she can't soothe, that you are fragile, and she has reason to worry about you. You try not to talk about your pills with her, and you try to make her see what you see in oxycodone the way you would a boyfriend of whom she disapproved. Considering all the time you spend tending to it, oxycodone might as well be your boyfriend. You love oxycodone like you've never loved a man. It's consistent and dependable and even amps up your dopamine production like an orgasm. You've taken stronger opioids (*see*: **Dilaudid, Methadone,** *and* **Opana**), but they don't target your headaches with oxycodone's precision, and they leave behind a dull pain like soap scum. That nagging residual ache stutters your concentration; it makes you miserable and irritable and mean. But on the right oxycodone dose under the right conditions, you can forget you have a headache, at least for a few hours. The doctors and pharmacy visits stress you out, but oxycodone makes your life worth living; oxycodone is worth disappointing the most important people in it. "I think they were really disappointed when you got back on those pills," the mom says when you tell her you wish you were closer to your sisters. She says it like your sisters' disappointment carries a weight equal to the pain in your head. Does no one think you're disappointed, too? You didn't choose your headaches. You chose oxycodone. Twice. You knew what taking it again would entail. Even including the pain and anxiety that accompanies **Withdrawal**, depending on oxycodone again is the hardest thing you've ever done. You know the way your family and friends and doctors will react, how the pills will circumscribe your life, and you choose to take them anyway. Oxycodone is the rational decision you make in irrational pain. Oxycodone is the only decision you have left.

Post-Acute Withdrawal Syndrome (*noun*): **1.** Constellation of symptoms that may appear after the acute withdrawal phase that follows cessation of regular alcohol, antidepressant, benzodiazepine, cocaine, opiate, and other substance use (*see also*: **Withdrawal**). Although not recognized by major medical associations or in the Diagnostic and Statistical Manual of Mental Disorders due to a paucity of scientific studies, post-acute withdrawal syndrome (PAWS) has been extensively reported by recovery communities, which have noted that PAWS may facilitate relapse. Symptomatology resembles that of mental illness in that symptoms recur in waves and fluctuate in severity. Common indications include anhedonia, anxiety, depression, emotional overreaction, emotional numbness, guilt, irritability, lack of initiative, obsessive-compulsive tendencies, panic, pessimism, and psychosocial dysfunction; cravings for the substance of choice; insomnia and other sleep disturbances; autonomic disturbances; impaired concentration, impaired memory, and impairment of interpersonal skills; increased sensitivity to pain and stress; problems with physical coordination; and trouble thinking clearly. Symptoms are physiologic manifestations of the brain relearning to enact chemical processes that the addictive substance previously initiated. PAWS typically abates with prolonged abstinence but can persist for months or years after detoxification. Intermittent recurrences or temporary worsening of symptoms may be triggered by anxiety, anger, fearfulness, frustration, or stress; other triggers include multitasking, social conflict, and unrealistically high expectations. **2.** "You've heard about PAWS, right?" your friend Brian asks. The two of you are sitting at the six-foot-long farmer's table in your mother's kitchen, its 100-year-old wood top pocked with icepick stabs. You dip raw snap peas, baby carrots, broccoli, and cauliflower into your mom's curry dip and King's Hawaiian rolls into Publix spinach dip while you compare detox notes. Brian and his wife Elizabeth got hooked on heroin in Memphis, which is where but not how they met. Now, they wake up before sunrise four mornings a week and drive 90 minutes to the methadone clinic in Pensacola because **Suboxone** throws Brian straight into withdrawal, and the clinic is about 80 percent cheaper than your Suboxone regimen. "PAWS like the cat shelter?" you joke. The only PAWS you know is the Panhandle Animal Welfare Society. During your senior year in high school, you met the volunteer-hour requirement for a state scholarship there. You filled food bowls and sifted cat shit from overused litter boxes and fell in love with all the lost causes. You tell Brian about Dottie, a one-eyed tortoiseshell you favored. He laughs and shows you a Wikipedia entry on his phone. You read aloud its long list of post-acute withdrawal symptoms and skim the other sections. "Years?" you ask. "Some people say it lasts forever," Brian says. "I'm sure I'll be one of them," you say and hand back the phone, defeated. "Want a cigarette?" Brian nods. He follows you onto the mom's big back porch that looks out onto the Choctawhatchee Bay. You take the cushioned rocking chair, and Brian sits in the matching wicker loveseat. He tells you what his counselor at the clinic told him about PAWS, his characteristic sped-up mumble miming your gathering fear. Over the eight months you spend on Suboxone, you'll visit that Wikipedia page a thousand times, memorize every one of the listed symptoms. You scour internet forums for others' accounts of post-acute withdrawal and sketch a timeline for your recovery, assuming you recover at all. You're a planner, and your detox is yet another event to plan: plan your days in the four-to-twelve-hour increments between Suboxone doses, plan your dosing-down process, plan to take no Suboxone dose on May 1. Plan how you'll spend the seven to ten days of acute withdrawal. Plan your move to Virginia. Plan on six months of PAWS, the longer end of its average length. Plan to demand less of yourself until November, when you'll be halfway into your first MFA semester. Still, PAWS surprises you. You mope around your mother's house and snap at the slightest provocation. A lump forms in your throat whether you're listening to Taylor Swift belt upbeat breakup songs or Jason Molina croon odes to endless depression. You cry any time you recognize an emotion in media: the feminine hunger in Susan Steinberg's short stories, all the striving on *Grey's Anatomy*, the outline of your body that a lover evokes in a song on his fourth album. Your anxiety hammers incessant and excessive, and your legs drag as if you haven't lost fifteen percent of your body mass. You lack any sense of forward momentum. Your brain sputters out within spitting distance of its destination. Your PAWS is more pronounced in Virginia, where you have to do your own grocery shopping and wash your clothes at the laundromat without a borrowed car. You stare at the syllabi for your classes. You have no idea how you'll meet their requirements: a twice-weekly response paper for the class that teaches you to teach freshman composition, a book a week for a seminar on Toni Morrison, online modules for a library-literacy course you don't need, three short stories for fiction workshop. You want to write the stories. The stories are why you're here. You detoxed for the stories, so that doctors and pills and pharmacies wouldn't take precedence over your writing. But the stories come out slowly and all wrong. You take four Advil to dim the fiery pain in the center of your head, sit down at your computer, and delete everything you type, smoking weed until you're too stoned to keep going (*see*: **Marijuana**). You take four more Advil to ease the ache that crept into your forehead while you stared at the white of your word processor and tell yourself you tried. You read until the natural light goes out, nap and masturbate, take four more Advil so you can binge-watch *The Americans* on your computer. "I'm bathing myself in narrative," you tell your friend Tom, whom you've asked to text you every morning *Are you writing? Are you writing?* until you answer *Yes, I'm writing*. You rarely have to admit you're not because Tom usually forgets to ask. You take three Advil to fall asleep. October turns to November, and your PAWS has waned just enough to confirm its persistence. You don't watch TV in the middle of the day anymore. You don't nap. You go to bed after *The Daily Show*, and you wake naturally at 6:00 or 7:00 instead of 5:00 a.m. (*see also*: **Withdrawal**). You make the guy you're fucking take Tom's place; Darren never forgets to ask if you're writing, and usually you are, but you can't get your characters to do anything. You have no interest in your characters even though your protagonists are mostly versions of you, barely fictionalized. You're in so much pain that it's hard to take an interest in anything but your body. Your palpitating heart still threatens to tear through your chest when you walk up the big staircase in the English building, and you're still faking it when you tell your mom you're fine, happy even. You're faking it after class with new friends, laughing as though you're not waiting to go home, where you can cry and beat up your brain for its glacial progress. You buy a new family-sized Advil bottle every two weeks, and still you always have a headache. Now you're sure you're one of the people for whom PAWS never ends. But you can't know. Your PAWS ends when you give your brain what it's wanted all year: opioids.

Prednisone (*noun*): **1.** Corticosteroid that prevents the body from releasing substances that cause inflammation. Sometimes used as an anti-inflammatory drug or immunosuppressant. Treats conditions including allergic, breathing, and skin disorders; arthritis and other inflammatory pain issues; and lupus. Adverse effects include behavioral or personality changes, bloody or tarry bowel movements, osteoporosis, severe upper-stomach pain, shortness of breath, susceptibility to infections and other communicable illnesses, and vision problems or eye pain. More commonly, prednisone may produce acne, bruising, dry skin, skin discoloration, and/or skin thinning; confusion, depression, and mood swings; dizziness or spinning sensation; high blood pressure; increased appetite, rapid weight gain, swelling, and bloating; increased sweating; nausea or stomach pain; pancreatitis; sleep problems; and headache. Patients must slowly reduce, or taper, their prednisone doses before discontinuing use. **2.** In the first year of your MFA, you aren't taking opioids. You're tossing ibuprofen, up to sixteen pills a day, at headaches that confine you to bed, keep you off your computer, convince you to give up the couple of beers you used to drink with peers after workshop. Your headaches draw you even further inward, where you find only pain and frustration. The Advil isn't working, but you stick with it. You don't think you'll ever take opiates again until you do. You go to Virginia Tech's Schiffert Health Center, tell a mildly cheerful older doctor about the migraines and intractable tension-type headaches, the oxycodone you used to take and the detox you completed nine months ago. You tell him about the Advil and the amped-up pain. He offers you hydrocodone. You don't have to lie or ask for it. He just gives it to you. You stretch eighteen pills over nearly thirty days, and when they're gone, you hold out for an extra week before requesting more. On your third visit, you settle for a prescription for codeine cough syrup (*see*: **Tussionex**) from a woman doctor who won't write you pills because, she says, you could die. You roll your eyes. "I used to take 300 milligrams of oxycodone in one day. I think I know how not to die," you say, but your expertise holds no weight. The clinic refers you to a neurologist in the next town over. The neurologist, a tall Puerto Rican man with a clipped, militaristic bedside manner, explains that your brain has learned to expect all the Advil you're giving it. "I'm addicted to ibuprofen?" you ask, incredulous. "I wouldn't say 'addicted,'" the neurologist says. "Your brain knows you're going to give it this chemical, and until you do, it produces pain." Now you know why your headaches have felt different lately, dull and stinging hot like a shot of whiskey: these are not your regular headaches. They're your regular headaches compounded by your brain's incessant begging for more and more ibuprofen. It's why, no matter how much Advil you throw at it, your head still burns for more: you've developed a **Tolerance** to an OTC pain reliever. The neurologist prescribes a prednisone taper. You're to take the steroid for three weeks, during which you're not allowed to take any kind of pain reliever at all except a $49 NSAID nasal spray that burns your nostrils but does absolutely nothing for your head. You are back in bed, rewatching *The West Wing* on Netflix in its entirety, eyes barely open and teeth bared like white knuckles. You spend spring break in New York, balled up on Tom's bed or couch while he drinks giant glasses of red wine and snorts cocaine so shitty and speedy that you don't even want any. Your heart is giant from the prednisone anyway. You talk too fast. You are sharp-edged and scattered and sad. You hurt all over. When you feel something, you feel it in triplicate because the prednisone renders you more sensitive than you already are. You have to spend the length of the taper in pain, and you were washed out and lonely before you got to the city. You rode thirteen hours each way on a crowded Megabus because Tom promised you three days of cuddling and talking and gentle fucking, but now he won't hold you when you sleep; it's uncomfortable, he says, which you take personally, as if he's saying you're uncomfortable, defective. He fucks you exactly once. You've been up all night and aren't expecting it. It's hard and fast and from behind, not at all the gentle lovemaking he used to lure you here. You feel anonymous and unloved, and you take it out on Tom for the next two days. You nag at him about the two inches he puts between your bodies when they could be touching and how he makes you walk to two bodegas in search of the perfect peppers to put in the chili he cooks before you catch your midnight return bus. He won't walk you, so you wander until you find it. When you're finally on the bus, you call and scream into his voicemail a list of everything he's done wrong. You spend your last three days on prednisone fidgeting and fighting with Tom over the phone until the two of you decide to quit talking. After the taper, you're too scared to take any Advil at all. The steroid was supposed to break your medication-overuse headache cycle, and you don't want to summon it back with the compound it learned to require. For about two weeks, your headaches are mild. But by May they're as intense and unrelenting as they were before you took the prednisone. You call Paul, the one man on whom you can still rely, to ask for **Elavil** again. You'll spend the three months between the end of the semester and your August 3 pain management appointment denying yourself NSAIDs four days out of the week, smoking weed in the afternoon, reading, writing nothing usable. It's like coming off Suboxone again, but now you can't remember why you agreed to the detox in the first place.

Suboxone (*proper noun*): **1.** Brand name of addiction-treatment drug composed of buprenorphine and naloxone. Buprenorphine, a partial opiate agonist, eases withdrawal symptoms and blocks full agonists from attaching to opioid receptors. The opiate antagonist naloxone is intended to prevent intravenous abuse and to expel full opiate agonists from opioid receptors, causing immediate withdrawal. Suboxone reduces cravings and discourages other drug use by eliminating the euphoria produced by opiate ingestion. Original tablet form, FDA-approved in 2002, discontinued in 2012 and replaced by sublingual Suboxone Film, which dissolves under the tongue and is believed to prevent tampering and deter injection. Though studies show near-identical success rates, Suboxone is marketed as an improvement on methadone maintenance treatment. The drug generated $1.55 billion in sales for manufacturer Reckitt Benckiser in 2012 alone. **2.** You will resist Paul's suggestion that you detox with Suboxone. You don't want to detox. Your oxys work for you. They do not cause you problems; pharmacists and stingy doctors cause you problems. But your non-stingy New York doctor will suggest that your beloved **Oxycodone** might exacerbate your pain, and you'll go home to Florida to test his theory. Paul promises support if you can't tolerate or simply dislike Suboxone, but your home state passes a law requiring that oxycodone prescriptions be written on a special pad that your New York doctor doesn't have and can't get before you'll go into **Withdrawal**. You call nearby doctors, hoping to stay on oxycodone while you apply to 21 MFA programs. No one cares about your MFA applications. No one cares about your headaches or your preferences. One doctor straight-up guffaws when you tell him how much oxycodone you take per day. "No one here is going to write you that," he says, and he's right. You'll resign yourself to Suboxone treatment. The clinic tells you to put six hours between your last oxycodone pill and your first Suboxone tab. You put nineteen, arriving raw and mean, in the earliest stages of withdrawal. You don't get the kind, moon-faced nurse who shares your name but the other one with a face like a pit bull fucked a horse and a voice like Alabama smoked a carton of Camels. You ask her what you're supposed to do about your pain, and she snaps at you to "Shut up. You're in withdrawal." She sits you in something like a dentist's chair and straps down your arms, as if it weren't humiliating enough to have a stranger hold open your mouth and stick a salmon-colored strip textured like a sandpaper/glassine hybrid under your tongue. The horse-faced nurse has to watch you take your first dose to ensure you're not allergic or starting too high. She disappears and reappears every few minutes to ask you questions you can't answer because a sublingual film strip is dissolving in your mouth, viscous and slimy. It tastes like licking an envelope laced with acetaminophen. When the strip is gone and you've been unstrapped, the nice nurse gives you water to swish and spit into the bathroom sink. Now that you're dosed and humbled, you're allowed into Dr. Jennings's office. He is round and clad in a red-plaid shirt and khakis and wire-rimmed glasses too small on his basketball of a head. Jennings treats you not like a pain patient but a drug addict. He shows no sympathy for your headaches. If you're still in pain after you habituate to Suboxone, he says, he'll rule out allergens and three other causation categories of which you can't keep track since you feel barely human. He outlines the process without regard to the months you'd spend in uncontrolled pain and doesn't tell you what he'd do to ease it. You assume nothing. Jennings prescribes you 60 Suboxone strips to take over 30 days. You left your insurance with your job in New York, so even with the coupon he proffers, your first month's supply costs over $600. But at least now you can dose yourself. You are diligent, placing the strips under your tongue exactly when you're supposed to: every four hours. By the third hour, withdrawal creeps into your bones, and you actually crave Suboxone even though the strips disgust you. You spend a week habituating to Suboxone itself and three days acclimating to your new, smaller dose each time you step it down. During those three days, you can't stop moving. You're constantly on the verge of exploding, of your heart blasting like a grenade through the rib cage you used to know a muscle couldn't break.

Topamax (*proper noun*): **1.** Brand name of the generic topirimate, an anticonvulsant first approved by the FDA in 1996 for epilepsy treatment. Commonly prescribed as a daily migraine preventive. Also used off-label in the treatment of borderline personality disorder; post-traumatic stress disorder; alcohol, cocaine, methamphetamine, and/or nicotine addiction; hypertension; cluster headaches; and antipsychotic-induced weight gain. Although its mechanism of action is poorly understood, Topamax remains the first-line treatment for migraine prevention, and studies show that about half of sample populations achieve at least 50 percent reduction in frequency and duration of migraine episodes per month; around 6 percent of patients report total relief. Patients are advised not to discontinue use before their sixth month, when Topamax reaches peak performance. Notorious for its side-effect profile, Topamax has earned the nickname "Dopamax" from adherents and detractors alike. **2.** You drop your purse on Paul's concrete floor and collapse into the leather chair across from his desk. "I can't take it anymore," you tell him. "I'll take the fucking Topamax." You can't say you've tried everything until you've tried

Topamax, so you've spent the past year trying everything else—**Acupuncture, Beta Blockers, Calcium Channel Blockers**, diet changes, **Elavil, Muscle Relaxers, SSRIs, Triptans**, vitamins—in an effort to avoid ever needing to try Topamax. On Topamax, you risk your life in a qualitatively different way than you do on **Oxycodone**. You could overdose if you took the three or five more oxys your headache wants, but the chance is slim. You'd have time to call an ambulance. Topamax probably won't kill you, but it may alter cognition, memory, language, speech, sight: all the things on which—as a writer, a storyteller, an obsessive steward of your own history—you depend for your sanity and survival. You see little point in slogging through your days without the ability to accumulate memories; to translate your experience into language; to craft narratives that shape the way you move through the world; to turn blank word-processor pages into physical spaces where you create, negotiate, interrogate your subjectivity. But you're so desperate that you will risk all these things for Topamax, for a head that doesn't hurt. Maybe grasping for words is worth that. You can't keep living the way you do, your head always aching, your eyes hidden behind sunglasses, your body so tired and confused by chemicals that you throw tantrums over missed trains and wrong turns, your boss's refusal to just have the goddamn *New York Times* delivered to his apartment because you're not a fucking secretary and just because you're always the first person in the office doesn't make it your job to pick the paper off the front step, the woman who won't roll her baby's gigantic stroller a few inches forward to let you on the subway. "What the fuck is wrong with you?" you scream at her. "Move, you goddamn cunt!" You asked nicely twice, but now the doors are shuddering, and the intercom is warning passengers to steer clear; you scream because you're terrified they'll close on your purse, rip it to shreds, send your pill bottles flying toward the tracks. The train will crush them, leaving shards of orange plastic next to tiny piles of pink and white powder for the rats to sniff around and devour. When you notice other passengers staring, you saunter to a new car as if you just can't stand to ride in the company of anyone too stupid to see the way this woman and her baby threatened your life. But you bear the worst of your cruelty. You berate yourself over every mistake you make at work, and you make too many. If you don't perk the fuck up, your friends will abandon you. You look like shit in your mirror, even in full make-up and your most reliable outfits: the black T-shirt dress with a tuxedo tail and sheer fabric down the side, the white tunic you bought on Etsy and wear when you feel bloated, the black sweater dress you put on over tights and vintage boots that makes you feel like Joan Didion. You're not the person you were when you bought those clothes, the one who'd beat back her childhood headaches and never fucked up or canceled plans, never got visibly angry or cried in public. Now you walk around New York wiping at tears and don't give a shit if other people notice. You growl at tourists for stopping in the middle of the sidewalk like you patrol the city. You flake on plans all the time and at the last minute. It's too hard to get in the shower, get in clothes, get on the train. Everything feels like a looming catastrophe. You are always lying: "Yes, I'm fine." "I had fun." "No, really, I'm fine." But you're not fine. You're fucked, and you're going to live your whole life in pain and despondence with the temper of a Greek god. Nothing is working. Not all the food you cut out of your diet. Not the acupuncture your shitty insurance doesn't cover or the psychotherapy appointments you attend on Wednesdays. Not the **Elavil** or the **Prozac** or the **Imitrex**. Nothing. "I'm so scared. I'm so fucking scared," you repeat while Paul prints the Topamax prescription. "You'd be kind of crazy if you weren't," he says. He reminds you that you probably won't get all the side effects you've read about. "Drug companies have to report anything anybody reports in the trials. Topamax is a serious drug. These are really sick people testing it. You don't know what someone would have felt anyway," he says.

"But stay off Google, okay?" You don't even look at the informatic that accompanies your prescription bottle. You are susceptible to the power of suggestion and don't want to give yourself the side effects. You take the pill every morning like you're supposed to. Mostly it makes your fingers tingle and your tongue slow and your brain flipping through its filing system audible. Once, about three months into your Topamax trial, you wake up without a headache. Even though the respite doesn't last, you take those few hours as a good sign. Another day, you only need seven oxys instead of ten. You and Paul write hopeful emails about Topamax that you'll find later and not recall composing. The side effects peak right before month six, the month when you'll know for sure that Topamax doesn't help. On your way home from work, a gorilla hand reaches out to grab your notebook on the subway. You pull it to your chest and check to see if anyone else saw the gorilla. But there is no gorilla on the train. The gorilla hand, the forty-something white man in the navy-blue suit under whose weight your smoke-break bench shifts, the black woman who sits next to you in her red-and-gold sari and disintegrates when you face her, the throbbing walls, the children as short as your shins are tall who circle your knees and evaporate when they try to climb into your lap: these are Topamax hallucinations. The apparitions feel as real as the exhaustion that follows their arrival. Your eyelids flutter closed, and you awake upright in your desk chair, unsure how long you slept and whether anyone noticed you dozing in your cubicle. At first you think you're taking too many oxys. You run tests: take eight pills on Monday instead of your usual ten, and still you fall asleep with your chin in your palm. More and more, you're losing the thread in conversations, losing words your fingers are poised to type. You'd have dealt with the visitations and the drowsy days, even the decline in your cognition, for another few weeks to see if Topamax gave you one more pain-free morning, but your vision starts to blur. You're zooming in 200 percent to read Word documents. Your nose nearly touches the computer screen as you try to interpret the hieroglyphs that populate your inbox. You succumb to Google. According to WebMD, Topamax can cause a rapid decline in eyesight, leading to total blindness. You email Paul. You can't go blind. You have to stop taking Topamax. But you can't just quit; you have to taper. You spend a week taking less and less of the drug you're scared will obliterate your ability not just to interpret the world but even to see it. And then you throw the pills in the trash, drug dispensation rules be damned. Coming out from under Topamax is like slinking into your own shed skin. It fits you better now. You no longer feel as though you'll burst out of it. You're the skinniest girl in New York, darting through crowds with an easy confidence you'd forgotten you possessed. Your synapses spark like firecrackers that never dim. You don't see chem trails or breathing walls anymore. You never see the gorilla, the woman, the man, or the children again. You see blue pills in orange bottles laid out across stacked calendars. "I'm not trying anything else for a while. I'm tired of being a guinea pig," you tell Paul. He says that's fine.

Triptans (*pl. noun*): **1.** Class of tryptamine-based abortive migraine drugs. Also used in the treatment of cluster headache. Tryptamine, as a non-selective serotonin-receptor agonist and serotonin-norepinephrine-dopamine-releasing agent, causes cranial blood vessels to constrict and inhibit the inflammation that characterizes some migraines and other headaches. Triptans' efficacy may also relate to their activation of serotonin receptors in nerve endings. Taken within 90 minutes of a migraine's onset, triptans abort attacks in 70–80 percent of patients with typical attacks. Less efficacious for those with atypical or unusually severe migraines, transformed migraine, or continuous migraine and for whom skin sensitivity accompanies migraine. Side effects include anxiety, blurred vision, changes in color vision, changes in hearing, changes in speech patterns and rhythms, chills, confusion, increased photophobia, insomnia, nightmares, stomach pain, sweating, trouble breathing, vertigo, recurrence of migraine, and headache. Patients taking antidepressant drugs may experience life-threatening serotonin syndrome. Fatal cardiac disturbances, seizures, cerebral hemorrhage, subarachnoid hemorrhage, and stroke have been reported. Patients should avoid taking triptans more than two or three times per week for both safety and efficacy. Sumatriptan, the first triptan brought to market, was approved by the FDA in 1993 following nearly 20 years of migraine research by the pharmaceutical company Glaxo. **2.** After her mother nearly dies from a sumatriptan-induced brain hemorrhage, you promise your friend Tricia that you won't take triptans. It's not a difficult promise to make. When you think of triptans, you remember an Imitrex ad from the early 2000s in which a woman pinches her forehead and looks up into the cinematographically enhanced headlights of a semi-truck. The ad made your head hurt, and then you felt guilty for identifying with the woman because your headaches, your pediatrician had told you, were "tension headaches," not migraines. Those lights still flash behind your eyes when you hear the word *triptan*. That triptans nearly killed Tricia's mom only bolsters your hatred of them. But you can't really avoid triptans. Neurologists insist you try at least one before they'll write your narcotics. You have to demonstrate that triptans don't work for you before you can establish yourself as an atypical patient. Your doctor in California gives you free samples of Imitrex. A neurologist in New York scoffs when you refuse his **Topamax** prescription and dismisses you with an exasperated sigh and a sample pack of Maxalt. Paul gives you Treximet once so that you can tell neurologists you've tried three triptans; that's what they want to hear. The sumatriptans make you sleep; when you wake up, you've still got a migraine, and you're too scared to take another, imagining Tricia's mother bleeding inside her skull. The Maxalt makes you feel like you're standing upside down. "I mean, I couldn't take that and go to work," you tell the doctor your insurance assigned you, aware that you sound crazy since you do go to work on 300 milligrams of **Oxycodone**.

Vicodin (*proper noun*): **1.** Narcotic analgesic used in the treatment of acute pain, moderate to severe. Contains hydrocodone (5, 7.5, or 10 mg) and acetaminophen (300 mg). Moved from Schedule III to the more restrictive Schedule II as of October 2014, a move that some attribute to the development of Zohydro, the first pure hydrocodone pill to make it to market. **2.** In California, you get your first identifiable migraine. It's 2008. You've parleyed your women's studies MA into a job with the ACLU's Drug Law Reform Project. The job is entry level. Easy work. Because you have the word "assistant" in your title, the ACLU has to pay you overtime if you stay past 5:00 p.m., so you're encouraged not to stay past 5:00 p.m. Your coworkers are laid back but professional: lawyers and legal assistants and legislative trackers, media strategists. You assist these people in doing good work, work you care about and of which you feel proud, but most of it is tedious. You book flights and collect receipts, track news stories and listen in on meetings. You're taking minutes during a conference call one afternoon when a pain crawls up the vertebrae at the base of your neck and settles behind your eyes; the pins and needles turn hard like nails hammered into the top of your skull, all angled rightward. You'll feel stupid going to urgent care for a headache. It's a headache. You've always gotten headaches. But your headaches have never felt the way this one does, like a mouthful of impacted wisdom teeth erupting through your brain. The urgent-care doctor writes you eleven 7.5 mg Vicodin. At first, you're triumphant—your own painkiller prescription!—but your enthusiasm dims as the migraine persists into days two and three. You go through the eleven pills by day four, and the urgent-care doctor calls you in a twenty-pill refill. The migraine lasts seven full days. But maybe this migraine is the best thing that's ever happened to you. Maybe you can use migraines the way your ex used his imaginary back problem. You could take the pills during your period, get high now and then. "I'm getting migraines that last a week," you picture yourself telling a doctor. "I can't sit in a dark room for a week, and I can't go to the ER twice a month." You'll pause there and wait for the doctor to offer you a monthly supply of whatever. You don't actually think you'll need it. You don't actually think the migraines will persist. You don't know they'll transform into disabling tension-type headaches or that over the next eight years you won't go a single day without one. You don't actually believe you'll end up in a physician's office in real need of a regular painkiller prescription until your physician indeed offers you **Butalbital with Codeine** when you give him that pause to fill.

Withdrawal (*noun*): **1.** Occurs upon cessation of physiologically addictive substances such as alcohol, nicotine, or opiates if patients establish dependence on said drugs. Symptoms of opiate withdrawal include loss of appetite and accompanying weight loss; abdominal cramping, nausea, vomiting, and diarrhea; anxiety and/or rapid heartbeat; yawning; low energy; insomnia; high blood pressure; hot/cold sweats; muscle pain; flu-like symptoms such as runny nose and teary eyes; dilated pupils and/or blurred vision; restlessness; and otherwise inexplicable mood changes including irritability, anger, agitation, and depression. In withdrawal, the dependent body relearns to function without opiates, which alter the way certain nerve receptors in the brain operate. Withdrawal symptoms represent those receptors returning to a "normal" state. Duration depends on drug of choice and mode of detoxification. Long-time opiate users generally experience more intense withdrawal symptoms than short-term users and are at greater risk for **Post-Acute Withdrawal Syndrome**. **2.** How is it the middle of May already? You wanted to have finished by now. You're moving to Virginia on July 1. If you're not off **Sub-oxone** by then, your mother will beg to stay with you in your adorable mid-century apartment until who knows when. And you hate to admit it since your mom has spent thousands of dollars on your doctors' visits and Suboxone strips, the food you peck at, the premium cable channels she doesn't watch, the gas you use to drive her car to work and therapy and Walgreens, but you're counting down the days until you leave your mom's house and move into your own. You wanted to quit Suboxone early enough to put three months between your last tab and the fall semester (*see also*: **PAWS**). Now, that's impossible. You stress and pack and plan. Now, you vow to quit by June 1. Your Suboxone dose isn't so low that you can quit taking it, but it's low enough that it offers no comfort. You're frantic all the time. You hate people and food and the TV, and you're always about to cry. You tell your boss at the Zoo Gallery, who's known you since you were born, that you can't handle your shifts anymore; you need to quit right now. "Your health is what's important," she says. You tell your psychiatrist that you need more **Klonopin**. Every time you see him, you need more Klonopin. Your heart won't stop thudding against your ribcage so hard it triggers panic attacks that trigger more panic attacks because you're panicked you'll have another panic attack. Your psychiatrist ups your Klonopin and ups your Klonopin. You're stepping down your Suboxone dose every other week and then every seven days. You rest at a quarter of a tab for three days. On the fourth day, before you're comfortable at a quarter, you take something between a quarter and an eighth. You start taking eighths on day five. Your Suboxone doctor said you should quit when you got down to a sixteenth of a strip. But how can you measure and cut a fucking sixteenth when the tabs aren't even an inch long? It's hard enough to fold the things into quarters and half those. Cutting a sixteenth proves impossible with your mom's bulky kitchen scissors, and her fingernail scissors aren't sharp enough. An eighth is as low as you'll go. An eighth is a quarter milligram of buprenorphine. That's got to be low enough. Your take your last pink sliver before you've habituated to eighths and move your leftover Suboxone upstairs, where you won't be able to reach it the next day. The next day, you're immobilized in the mom's bed. Your days carry the distinct smell you associate with staying home sick from elementary school: the usually absent scent your house emits, your own hot breath on your unwashed skin, chicken noodle soup and Saltine crackers and Coca-Cola. You've always been small, but in detox you are doll-sized beneath blankets that feel more substantial than you do; you need all your strength to kick them off when you flash hot and pull them back to your chin when you get cold again. Your mom lifts the edges of her comforter off the carpet and pulls taut the sheets you've ravaged with your restless limbs because you can't. You are weak, needy, helpless. Childlike. The television dwarfs you. Even pushing buttons on the remote control drains your stamina. You hold onto the wall and the doorjamb to make the thirteen-step trek to the bathroom; sometimes you make the return trip on your hands and knees. Your legs ache to the center of your bones. Your bowels gurgle. Your stomach cramps and crepitates. Your head throbs. Even your teeth feel transparent and exposed. Everything turns to fuzz and confusion. You don't sleep. You take Advil. Advil, Advil, Advil, Advil. You take extra **Clonidine** to make yourself drowsy, but you're still up to take in *The Daily Show*'s "Moment of Zen," the entirety of *The Colbert Report*, Jimmy Fallon's *Late Night* monologue. You take your time eating since food turns your stomach. The mom takes the time to list for you the contents of the refrigerator, and you take to nodding and gritting your teeth so you won't yell at her like an ingrate brat. Without your mom, you'd have had to detox alone, cold turkey, or hitch rides with Brian to the methadone clinic, which would have taken time you don't have. You're in a rush. You don't know that rushing means hurling yourself toward more fog and mental disarray, more anxiety, more pain, months that feel like those three days after you lowered your Suboxone dose (*see also*: **PAWS** *and* **Suboxone**). Before you leave Florida, you give your unused Suboxone to Brian's friend who wants to stop shooting **Heroin** but can't afford the doctors' fees. You never want to see those blue-and-white packets again, but you'll find them, months and even years later, in pants pockets and at the bottom of your purse, where you carry the blue octopus Paul crocheted for you before you left New York. Its tentacles, he said, represented the freedom you'd experience when you cast off your narcotic dependency. You don't know that in a year you'll place yourself back inside that opiated prison. But you'll still carry Paul's octopus in your purse, pausing now and then to squeeze its bulbous head and wrap yourself in your New York doctor's magnanimity. Your purse is not a safe place. Books and pens, umbrella handles and student papers, receipts and everyday detritus jab at the octopus's eyes and rough up its delicate skin; water leaks on its head. That the octopus has survived four years in such inclement conditions reminds you that you are just as tough. Its eight arms and smiling head tell you you're not really alone because, for every night you spent in front of the TV or behind a book, Paul spent one crocheting this sea creature to commemorate your departure. You made Paul believe in your pain and even your treatment preferences, so you can make another doctor believe you, too. You wait almost six months to admit to Paul that you're back on **Oxycodone**. *You know I don't subscribe to recovery dogma*, he emails back, *but be careful*. That Paul isn't disappointed grants you permission to recast the octopus's tentacles. Now, they reach toward all the things you can do because you granted yourself permission to get back on a painkiller that works.

DENIAL

1. On December 23, 1984, the *Northwest Florida Daily News* dedicated a full-page spread to the arrival of the Long triplets. "Babies Brighten Season of Joy," reads the headline on page 1C. Under it, a subheading states that Beth, Chelsea, and I are "beautiful gifts at [the family's] Destin home." My sisters and I were born at Sacred Heart Hospital in Pensacola, Florida, exactly 86 days before the article's publication. The doctors said we were identical. The newspaper said the same. The mom says that, before her OB put her on bed rest, strangers would walk up to her in the grocery store and, when they learned she was pregnant with triplets, ask if she'd taken fertility drugs. So did the paper. "Neither parent knows of any multiple births in the family history," writes Living Today section editor Peggy May, adding that the mom "took no fertility drugs." The article centers on our lives at home and the changes we'll cause in our parents' routines; it provides descriptions of our emerging personalities and matching pink dresses, which look white in the four accompanying gray-scale photos. The sole full-color picture shows the mom feeding one of us from a bottle while the other two—even I can't tell us apart—squirm in one of our three identical cribs. The mom sports shoulder-length bobbed hair and short, side-swept bangs. Her brown roots blend into dyed-blond ends. A swipe of purple shadow is visible on her eyelids. Two black-and-white photos show the mom cradling us in her lap, a Madonna and Three-Headed Child. She gazes down at the creatures she birthed, the look on her face as soft as

her eyelashes. At the bottom of the page, the three of us lie in our playpen like unfurled pill bugs. "Little Amy," as May describes me, reaches one hand toward the camera and turns her face toward "medium-sized" Chelsea, who places one hand on Amy and gropes with the other for "the largest baby," Beth. Against a white-blanket backdrop, we look like we're falling. Chelsea's spread limbs stretch in a sort of starfish shape. Beth's giant head, so large it put eight minutes between our births, faces both the photographer and Chelsea. She holds up her hand as though to push away the camera or to grab hold of something more familiar. Between Chelsea and me lies one of two crocheted Raggedy Ann dolls. Beth squashes the third with her body; its striped socks and black booties poke out beneath her gown. The dolls are there to show how small we are. In a picture captioned "DADDY'S HOME FOR LUNCH TODAY," the mom looks somewhere past the camera, toward but not at the dad, who holds one of our miniature hands in his. We are sleeping in the mom's lap. Only because the caption notes the date on which I left the hospital do I know that I am furthest from the dad, who tells me that when I was born he could hold me in the palm of one hand. In this picture, the dad's hand looks giant. His hair is floppy, a bit Beatles-esque, and he smiles down at us so the viewer can't make out any feature but his nose, which my sisters and I share. The dad cuts a dark figure beside the mom with his mop of richly pigmented hair and permanently tanned skin (he worked for years as a life-guard before he married the mom and joined his father's insurance agency). He wears a tan suit and a navy-blue or black necktie. In all these pictures, the mom has on a long-sleeved white dress with subtle shoulder pads and a necklace I know is gold because I can still feel its fish-scale texture on my curious-child's fingertips. She looks angelic. The dad looks awed. And we sleep or yawn or draw out our arms like wings, a jumbled trio of white-gowned babies with our mother's giant eyes and open mouth.

2. Theoretically, my sisters and I have identical DNA, but neither Beth nor Chelsea has headaches like mine. I'm aberrant. If I asked a geneticist, I know he or she would tell me that genes express themselves differently in different people even if those people are identical triplets. I remember doing Punnett squares in high school, solving for the different phenotypes produced by sets of dominant and recessive traits. A cousin on the mom's side gets daily headaches. The dad's mom suggests I stand in a hot bath; it was her mother's migraine remedy. Our family tree sprouts a headache-ridden leaf on each side, but none of the family headaches exactly resembles mine. Since the pain in my head has little if any genetic determinant, sometimes I think the fault must lie somewhere in me. As doctors and therapists, family members, friends, and lovers have all suggested, I'm wound too tight; if I could just loosen up, they say, maybe I wouldn't get headaches. But placing the blame on me is lazy and, I sometimes think, cruel: a way to designate "Little Amy" a deviation from the norm. Unlike most people, "the norm" is not, for me, an abstract set of societal standards to which I'm theoretically held. My norms are embodied. They are Beth and Chelsea, and Beth and Chelsea don't get headaches or panic attacks or take narcotics for pain and anxiety disorders they escaped by birth order. The norm is health and stability. Since I can claim neither, there must be something abnormal about me. Because—just look!—there are three of her, and the other two aren't floundering in pain and polluting their bodies with oxycodone.

3. The mom's OB in Fort Walton nearly killed her for the bragging rights to our birth. He postponed sending his patient to the better hospital in Pensacola because he wanted to say that he had ushered the Long triplets safely into the world. Our long-time pediatrician told the *Daily News* that the statistical chance of birthing triplets at the time was 1 in 100,000. He said

it happened, "in this area, about once every 10 years." We came too early. We came fragile. We stayed in the neonatal intensive care unit for so long—Beth until October 22, three weeks after our late September birthdate; Chelsea until Halloween; and me until November 19—that our nurses all remembered the mom when she attended one of their retirement parties more than two decades later. The parents couldn't decide on names, so the nurses at Sacred Heart called us Baby A, Baby B, and Baby C; it's why we're named Amy, Beth, and Chelsea. Historically, people name their babies early to prevent death or to guarantee entrance into heaven, as if a name constitutes a soul. To our doctors, our tiny bodies trussed up in tubes needed saving first. When I reveal myself as a triplet, the person first learning of Beth and Chelsea usually jokes that maybe "*That's* why you're so skinny! Your sisters ate all the food!" Sometimes I think this is partially true: my sisters tried to kill me for my share of our womb's resources. It's not that farfetched. Twins sometimes eat each other in the womb. Or, more accurately, as Beth has explained, they "transfuse." One's blood supply gets redirected to the other, and if it happens early enough, the demised twin shrinks and disintegrates. Maybe I was supposed to have been the demised triplet. Paul once said that my headaches are probably vascular. Maybe my sisters drained the blood supply in preparation for my transfusion into their bodies, and so my veins didn't develop right. Maybe my headaches are punishment meted out by a universe that never wanted me in it, the pain my penance for surviving my sisters' attempts to draw me into them with their forming fingers.

4. Beth is an OB now. She completed her residency in the summer of 2015 and moved to the Midwest to start a fellowship in gynecological oncology. Beth says that naturally occurring triplets are too rare; we are not among their ranks. According to my doctor sister, only she and Chelsea are identical.

I'm the fraternal triplet, she says. I admit I don't look as much like my sisters as they look like each other. I never have. When I lived in New York, I saw a therapist who'd done her doctoral research on multiples. I relayed to her a memory from sometime before my sisters and I started kindergarten: We are competing in a race around the house, and I not only lose but feel in some intangible way distanced from Beth and Chelsea. The distance I perceive is not the physical or temporal distance we put between each other as we circled the one-story ranch house where we lived then. The house wasn't that big. I can't have lost by more than a few seconds, a few feet. The distance is an emotional distance: isolation, alienation, an otherness for which I can't account. I couldn't define it for my therapist, and I can't define it for myself now. But I can picture Beth and Chelsea huddled together, giggling under a framed New Orleans Jazz Fest poster as if plotting some conspiracy, and I feel again that bitter, bewildering pang that greeted me at the wall we'd designated our finish line. This memory may be my earliest. I'm not sure. I remember my childhood the way I remember certain nights before I quit drinking. My memories clump together, disperse, and lose their context like pictures never put into an album. Beth calls this sort of memory "low frame count." We use the phrase to refer to those snapshot moments you recall after a night spent not completely black-out drunk but close enough. For all I remember of it, I might as well have spent my first decade on the planet totally wasted. My therapist kept coming back to that memory of the race, as though I've constructed my relationship to my sisters, to the whole goddamn world, around it. Maybe I have. I don't know. I don't know any more than I know whether my sisters and I are identical. But when Beth picked me out as the fraternal triplet, I could see why. For 30 years, I've felt in some tangled, inexplicable way set apart from them.

5. Beth and Chelsea think I have a drug problem. Beth is convinced that soon I'll be back on the 300-milligram oxycodone dose I took daily in New York. That I've spent a year back on oxycodone and am only at 40 mg makes no difference to her. She shrugs when I say I know I took too much back then and that I don't want to—I can't—get my dose up that high again. When I finish my MFA, I'll move and have to convince another doctor to write my prescriptions; the lower I keep my dose, the more easily I'll replace my Blacksburg supplier. Beth thinks I should exercise, quit smoking, dedicate my body to doctors eager to experiment with new treatments. In medical matters, Beth's opinion always carries more weight than my experience because I go to doctors and she is one. For Beth, my headaches are a medical issue. For Chelsea, my headaches are a moral quandary or a psychological problem. "I meant," she said when I confronted her about the only time she's spoken of my pain and the drug I take to alleviate it, "that I'm sorry you *feel* like you need that stuff." To Chelsea, I only *feel like* I need opiates. I suffer from a false consciousness born of my love for narcotics; I want opiates, but I don't need them. It's a narrative a lot of people like to foist on me: I use my headaches as an excuse to abuse drugs I like. That I've addicted myself to oxycodone to numb a pain Chelsea thinks I could and should relieve with ibuprofen is a measure of how weak I am, how off-kilter my moral compass. She doesn't have Beth's medical knowledge, but she inherited the dad's penchant for pro-claiming himself inherently correct and anyone who disagrees with him an idiot. I'm sure Chelsea thinks I'm a baby about pain; that headaches can't be this bad; that I should just, as she likes to say when presented with any complex or intractable dilemma, "deal with it."

6. The *Daily News* article reports our weights and heights at birth and at the time of publication. When I erupted from the mom's overworked uterus,

I weighed a full pound less than my three-pound sisters and measured two inches shorter. Three months later, I weighed five pounds; Beth and Chelsea weighed, respectively, seven and six (again May identifies Beth as "the largest baby," which struck my largest sister as a barb when the mom framed and hung the article on a wall adjacent to the laundry-room door). In old pictures, I can usually pick myself out by identifying the smallest one of us, but not since we were infants have we been all that difficult to tell apart. "Though the girls are identical, they can be told apart now," May writes not quite three months after our births. She even states my abnormality outright: I'm the firstborn yet the smallest. "It is more likely for the firstborn to be the largest," May reports. I never caught up to my sisters in size. Even now, my body is shorter and thinner. My sisters aren't fatter than I am; they're just bigger. I lack their muscle definition and tanned skin. Even their faces are bigger than mine, broader. In pictures, I look invariably younger, like I'm waiting to hit puberty. It's as if my bones themselves are too small. Side by side, my sisters might be giants and I a bird.

7. Chelsea lives in Destin and works as an attorney. It's what she always said she wanted to do: get a bachelor's degree in something—anything—and move on to law school; after she obtained her juris doctor, she wanted to move back to Destin and marry Jack, whom she'd been dating since our senior year in high school. Chelsea majored in psychology and minored in art history, and when she graduated from law school, she had a job waiting in Destin with the lawyer for whom she'd interned during summer breaks. Chelsea married Jack on May 28, 2009, under a fat oak tree on the grounds of Eden State Park in Walton County. She wore an elegant white dress, the silhouette minimalist but for the big bow beneath her small breasts. Chelsea's wedding attire suited her exactly: a modern design that incorporated traditional elements, stylish and

timeless, elegant yet fun. She looked like she'd stepped off a page in a bridal magazine. Each of us bridesmaids—Beth, Christina, Joanne, Leah, Rebecca, Taylor, and I—wore the same knee-length halter dress, tailored to our proportions and embellished with a bow in the back, but we got to choose our shoes. I bought a pair of stiletto sandals that cost more than my COBRA health-insurance premium. Their bronze T-strap, attached to a matching ankle clasp, sloped down my foot toward thin silver, pewter, bronze, and gold arches that spread out over my toes; in the back, another bronze stem sprouted from the bright-gold triangle that secured my heel. I didn't have a job anymore, so I needed footwear that would act as armor. It sounds selfish, but at my sister's wedding, I worried most about how I would reply to people who asked what I was doing. Beth was in medical school. Chelsea was the bride. I could only protest that it wasn't my fault I'd lost my job at the ACLU or that in four months I hadn't procured a replacement. I planned out an answer to every question someone might pose to me. The mom said no one would ask any; they'd focus on Chelsea. But when so many people who know you in so many different ways and to such varying degrees converge in one place, they can only talk about the bride for so long. At some point, everyone with whom I spoke asked what I was doing. I didn't go into detail. I said I was in California and had no idea where I'd be next. I laughed at myself. I swallowed barbiturate-and-codeine pills with red wine and leaned into the idea that my life is a running joke. Beside Beth's and Chelsea's immanently sensible, respectable, real lives, mine will always look scattered and fanciful, like a sketch of a life I'll eventually have to fill in with something practical and adult—something real. During the ceremony, I read a passage from the same copy of *The Velveteen Rabbit* that the mom used to read to us when we were kids. The Skin Horse is explaining to the titular rabbit that toys become real through the love of the child who plays with them. *Does it happen all at once?* the rabbit asks. The Skin

Horse says no. *It takes a long time. That's why it doesn't happen often to people who break easily, or have sharp edges, or who have to be carefully kept. Generally, by the time you are Real, most of your hair has been loved off, and your eyes drop out and you get loose in the joints and very shabby. But these things don't matter at all, because once you are Real you can't be ugly, except to people who don't understand.* I cried while I read it. The guests, every one of them, cried in their rented white folding chairs. People kept coming up to me at the reception to gush about how much my reading had touched them. I thanked them and did not say that, when I cried, I did not cry because—or, not entirely because—the passage offered such a heart-rending parallel to the love that Jack and Chelsea shared. I cried because, if Margery Williams's Skin Horse is right, I am not real and may never become so. My sharp edges must be carefully kept, managed with the right pills and the right foods, with dimmed lights, low voices, rest. I break down in doctor's offices and grocery store aisles; I break down in pain or for no reason at all. I broke down at my sister's wedding because I'd never felt the love I meant, through the Skin Horse, to describe to the people watching Chelsea and Jack say their vows. I cried because I didn't think I ever would and had no reason to think otherwise.

8. I didn't mean to tell Beth I'd gotten back on opioids. I was telling her a story that ran right into the pills. "Oh, shit," I said and paused. "If I tell you this, will you promise not to tell Chelsea?" Beth promised. "I'm taking opiates again," I said. "No. Amy!" she said. She begged me to stop before I got dependent. She rattled off statistics and medical guidelines that warn against long-term opioid use for chronic head pain. She cried. Beth never cries. When we got off the phone, she called the mom. I know because, when the mom finished talking to Beth, she called me in tears, boiling with anger. By the time I hung up the phone, we were both pissed at Beth for having upset the status quo, in which

the mom accepts my opioid use and we don't discuss it unless we have to. Over the first Christmas break since I'd started taking oxys again, Chelsea caught me in her condo's parking lot with David, who'd wanted to see me while I was in town and had a Lortab to give me. "Whatever," she said, a snarl in her voice. "I know you're taking those pills again." She uttered *those pills again* in the same tone she used later to dismiss my hurt feelings. She said it as though taking them makes me a criminal, as if I do it not to relieve real pain but because I want to feel the high I can't reach unless I take an entire day's dose at one time. I couldn't see her face, but I pictured her holding her phone to her ear, mascara-coated eyelashes fluttering above her rolling brown irises, which match mine. I was in the median in front of her apartment building, trying to make a U-turn back toward the mom's house and also hang up on my sister before she hung up on me. I couldn't get my finger on the red End Call button fast enough, so I told her to fuck off and called her a cunt. It's a terrible thing to say about one's sister and, worse, I meant it. I threw my phone so hard it banged against the mom's passenger-side window and fell between the seat and door. I had to pull into another condo's parking lot to dig it out in case Chelsea called to proffer the apology on which I'm still waiting.

10. In the *Daily News* article, May writes that the mom "emphasizes that the girls already have different personalities" and that both she and the dad "are determined that they'll be individuals, not just 'the triplets.'" Still, people usually greet the news that I'm a triplet with an exclamation-marked "There's three of you!" There are not three of me. There is one Amy Lorraine Long and two other people who look a lot like her. When my sisters and I applied to college, the dad watched his friends pressure their children into attending their own alma maters. He acted bemused and dismissive. "I don't need to create a bunch of mini-mes. I want you to do what you want to do," he told us.

Yet, when I make a decision he doesn't like, the dad forgets he's ever said this. When I got a job with the ACLU, he called me a communist. When I said I wanted to live in D.C. proper instead of its suburbs, he said, "No one *chooses* to live in that city. People live in the city because they *have* to," as if it were still the 1980s. He claims he could have withstood the pain I bury under opioids. (I haven't told him I'm taking them again. I don't want to hear my father call me a junkie.) I did not expect he'd support my decision to go back to school, but he has. Maybe because the state pays my tuition and offers me health insurance and a livable stipend, and the dad doesn't really know that a master's of fine arts in creative writing prepares me to do almost exactly nothing, that there's no specific job waiting for me when I graduate. Or maybe he's resigned himself to never agreeing with what I do. Maybe he's given up on me the way I've given up on curing my headaches or on making him understand them.

11. Chelsea isn't married anymore. I saw Leah, Chelsea's former best friend and the woman Jack is with now, at our friend Kevin's funeral over the summer. Kevin overdosed, presumably on heroin; his family kept it quiet. No one addressed Kevin's drug use except his closest friend, Adam, who pulled me aside after the service and asked for a list of harm-reduction organizations. Adam was planning a Kickstarter campaign to raise money for Kevin's family and wanted to donate any leftover funds to nonprofits whose efforts might have saved his friend. He'd send books of Kevin's poetry to anyone who contributed. I hadn't even known Kevin wrote poetry, but I knew he wrote songs; his brothers had played two of his compositions during the ceremony, and he'd written one to play for Leah when he asked her to marry him a decade earlier. She'd given back the ring—a toenail-sized diamond on a pewter band, smaller diamonds encrusted around it like a metallic moat—when she broke off their engagement, but to Kevin's memorial service, Leah wore the pearl necklaces

he'd given her, all of them knotted together the way I've seen sorority girls wear theirs. I'd taken a 2-milligram Klonopin and a 10-milligram oxy on my drive to the church, but seeing her still turned my knees to gelatin. ("If she talks to me," I told the friends I sat down beside, "I'll drag her out behind the church and bash in her head with my shoe." I held up my foot, brandishing one of my five-inch wedge heels.) Leah interrupted her conversation with someone I didn't recognize to smile at me and say "Hi" in the voice of an innocent, hand held up as though hailing a friend she hadn't seen in a long time. I contorted my face into its best withering look and said, "Not today." I swatted the air between us and walked past her without meeting her eye or missing a beat. Beth says I can't blame Leah for Jack and Chelsea's divorce, and I don't. My sister and her ex-husband were unevenly matched in ambition and in the intentionality with which they lived their lives. They loved each other, but the third party probably only sped up a vehicle that would have crashed anyway. I should have been but wasn't there for Chelsea during her divorce. I was in New York. I barely remember if we even talked on the phone. I didn't do anything but change Leah's name to *Sister-Fucking Husband-Stealing Cunt* in my cell phone's contacts list and ignore her pleading text messages. I regret that I left it to the rest of Destin to console and protect my sister, but I don't know what I could have done that her friends didn't. Almost no one in town would speak to Leah or Jack, and she got kicked out of bars even when Chelsea wasn't in them. I'm not even sure my sister would have confided in me over the phone or accepted whatever help I might have offered her. I'm even less sure I would have deserved it if she had.

12. May distinguishes my sisters and me in her article not only by our sizes but by the sounds we make when we cry. Beth's, she writes, "is quite lusty." Chelsea's is "consistent." She characterizes mine as "short, abbreviated but

insistent." I don't want to say that a newspaper editor predicted our person-alities by listening to us wail as newborns. But Beth, if not necessarily "lusty" in the way one typically thinks, conducts her life with a zeal that I worry is missing from mine. She seems to like life, to think of it not as a slog or a burden but a maze she can navigate on her own terms. When we were kids, she refused to ask waiters or women who worked in department stores for directions to the bathroom. She wanted to find it without help, and she felt embarrassed when she couldn't. She doesn't like to impose on people. She'd rather charge ahead and pretend she's sure than admit defeat or insecurity. The description of Chelsea as a "consistent" crier strikes me as the most prescient. Chelsea has always known what she wanted, and she's still confounded by people who don't. She lives consistently; after her marriage ended, her life changed completely, but it also didn't change at all. I don't know what to say about May's characterization of my cry except that it sounds strange, out of place. May uses not one but three adjectives, all of them neutral, as if my cry is not describable in any pleasant way. And the article about us is nothing if not pleasant. Our nursery is pleasant and sunbathed. Our parents are pleasant and unbothered by what must have amounted to staggering stress; we are a "family of five plus pet" that, it seems, "has always been in place." Even our mess—the pile of car seats and high chairs on the kitchen table—May renders in the pleasant tones of a flight attendant. But in hindsight there's something off about the article. May asks the mom why we have three of everything but only a single playpen. "We hope they'll be able to play together in this one!" the mom says. The quote comes off as reassuring after the paragraphs devoted to our distinct attributes. We're still "the triplets" sometimes. Yet May assesses the differences in our bodies, our cries, the amount of formula we each drink (a formula manufacturer sponsored our diet; I'm not sure what we gave it in return) as if she's comparing horses at auction. If you slant your eyes at it, the article implies that we were pitted against each other from the start.

13. Our friend Ahmed set me apart from my sisters in high school. He gave me a nickname: Cheese. It's the only nickname that's ever stuck to any of us. Ahmed said I ate my food like a rat, which he thought was funny because I didn't like cheese; the name made sense at the time. Before he was my best friend, I dated Ahmed for a month in ninth grade. We shared my first kiss at the back of the Pensacola Civic Center during a Green Day concert. We didn't care about Green Day in 2002. Ahmed bought tickets to the show so we could watch The Get Up Kids open. I'd been thinking about breaking up with Ahmed for a week or so, which felt like forever in high-school time. Chelsea told me to wait until we started making out. "Then you'll like it," she said. I waited for the making out to happen, and then I had to wait an extra week to break up with Ahmed so he wouldn't think I'd used him for concert tickets. I couldn't tell him I was breaking up with him because his kiss had felt like sucking on a wet washcloth. I broke up with him over the phone. I didn't want to do it at school and upset him in front of other people. He took the news like a champ and then called back sobbing. "Taylor!" he cried. I put my hand over my mouth and winced. "I'm sorry. This is me again," I said. Taylor's number was two digits off from ours. Ahmed and I still talk on the phone, and he still calls me Cheese. We have friends who refer to me only as Cheese. One friend will say, "Hey, Cheese," and another will look at him as one might a maniac. We explain the confusion, and the uninitiated friend pretends to get it, pretends to understand the weird inside-joke logic my nickname carries. I say I don't mind it, and I don't. But I sort of wish the people I've known longest didn't introduce me as a joke.

14. In the mom's garage, I found the notebook that my sisters, Leah, Rebecca,

and I passed in and out of one another's lockers so we could organize our "band" business. Rebecca and I were supposed to play guitar, Beth bass, and Leah drums. Chelsea would sing. But none of us was good enough to actually write songs or perform them, even in a Ramones-style punk band. Pages of the notebook are dedicated to Leah's inability to procure a drum set, and when we plan our practices, we remind her to bring her sticks so that she can, as I write in one entry, *practice banging on things to a beat*. We spend more time planning the pictures we'll put on the Geocities site I designed: us in ratty public bathrooms or school hallways wearing black T-shirts, jeans, and Converse, the Joey Ramone uniform only I actually donned. In the notebook, when I'm not complaining that *ugh, my head is killing me*, I beg the others to send me the bios I need for the webpage. Our endeavor was less about music than identity. Through the band, we attempted to embody and display the selves we wanted to be, to become, to create. We kept an envelope in the back for the lyrics we wrote, mostly mine and Rebecca's anti-establishment credos and barbs at the mean girls against whom we defined ourselves. Years later, when Chelsea got divorced, the only girls left to befriend in Destin were the same girls we called out in our "songs." She quit inviting me out with them years ago. Chelsea knows I don't want to go—and not only · because my head can't take the high volumes their voices reach when they get together to guzzle migraine triggers in bars or on the dad's boat. I don't like these girls. It's uncomfortable to hear people who make enough money to joke about it complain that they don't have enough or to listen to their careless ignorance of all the other things a person might need in order to feel comfortable in the world. They don't read or engage deeply with ideas, with art or music or cultural discourses. In their conversations, they relive last weekend's blackouts and talk about the girlfriend with whom one segment of the group is fighting. They buddy up to the staff at their favorite bars. They tip well. They aren't cruel to outsiders, but they are a closed loop into which a new person has to throw elbows to insert herself. When I'm with Chelsea's friends, I end up in that lonely zone between conversations: three of them joke about one's maxed-out credit card, a husband narrates his day at work to another girl's boyfriend, four people are talking about something I can't hear over the other voices around me. They talk over one another, over music and clinking glasses, so often that their "inside voices" have become shrill and hoarse even when no one needs to yell. But these girls also cared for my sister when I couldn't or wouldn't or just didn't. I'm grateful to them for that. Maybe Chelsea has to be one of these girls to get along in Destin. Or maybe she finally feels like herself with them the way I thought I did with David.

15. I cannot write fairly about my sisters. I write about Chelsea's divorce, the betrayal she endured, but barely touch upon the pain it caused her. I let my anger take over the page. I move right to the story's end and write about Chelsea the way I see her now: gregarious, loved, smug, smiling beside girl-friends and fiancés. I forget that her life hasn't gone as planned, either. I never step back to admire the kindness Beth shows her patients or the daring with which she handles the lives in her hands; I say nothing of the loneliness she expresses to me, our shared worry over whether we'll find men with whom to spend our lives. I complain about the way she uses her medical knowledge against me but ignore the student loan debt she accrued to acquire it. I'm consumed by my pain, and I've stopped listening to my sisters' sides of the story. I have to. Ignoring them protects me from their accusations and lets me retain my role as the persecuted one. In the stories I tell about my sisters, I am always the sister who is slighted, the one who doesn't fit; I'm belittled and othered, Cinderella lacking her glass slipper. I know that's not right. I should have more empathy. What if I looked at my sisters and saw not the ways

they've exacerbated my pain but the pain I've inflicted on them? If Beth and Chelsea won't acknowledge that their concern and judgment hurts me, I tell myself, I shouldn't have to consider their fear or disappointment. I know their misgivings are rooted in the way they love me, but I want them to love me, to like me, as I actually am and not as they wish I were. I want them to think about headaches and opioids in the same ways I do.

16. In the *Daily News* article, there is a right way to raise triplets, and the parents are following it. The mom spends all day feeding us and two hours giving the three of us baths. We are amply provided for by our parents; by a baby-feeding corporation; by our maternal grandmother, who sewed a unique quilt for each of us; by the neighbors and friends and extended family who, according to May, showered us with "handmade pillows, clothing, and every imaginable other accessory and cuddly toy." The parents are attuned to our needs as growing people. We are taken to the doctor. We are read books. We are sisters, a unit, but individuals, too. May writes in a cheery voice without straying from the "just the facts" framework that used to characterize, apparently, even newspapers' lifestyle sections. If there is a right way to raise triplets, there is a right way to write about them, and May cuts that down to an art, a sweet science that smells like sweat and talcum powder.

17. My inability to write fairly about my sisters is not dishonest. It's a failure of will. It's self-protection. If I softened my edges, let Beth and Chelsea rub me bare, where would that leave me? I love my sisters. I recognize the things they do that bother me and the things they do that are kind, funny, honorable—admirable, even. I can acknowledge that part of the problem lies in my rigidity and all the ways I let my headaches dictate what I will and can do. Beth and Chelsea have their own answers. They hold ideas about me, my

headaches, and the drugs I take that I think are unfair, and I make assertions about the way my sisters treat me that they would surely deem the same. When we were little and the dad read *The Runaway Bunny* to us, he'd replace the *mother rabbit* printed in the book with "daddy rabbit." My sisters and I always groaned in unison. "But she's wearing a dress," we'd protest, pointing at the mother rabbit illustrated in her hoop skirt and apron. "Who's telling the story?" the dad would say. I'm telling this one.

TISA'S MOTEL:
INSTRUCTIONS & SECURITY

INSTRUCTIONS

1. Knock on door and wait for David to answer.
2. Step into room. Smell stale cigarettes and dirty sheets. Feel weirdly glamorous and a little scared. You're not supposed to be here.
3. Stay just long enough that your parents will believe you when you tell them you were hanging out with your high school friends, who don't take methadone and narcotic anti-anxiety pills.

FOR YOUR SECURITY

*   Keep your valuables in your bag. Keep your phone on hand in case your mom calls.
*   Secure deadbolt. Remove your clothes and crawl under dirty sheets. For a long time, do nothing that requires you remove your clothes, or at least not *all* of them. Wait months to reciprocate after David goes down on you. Achieve your first orgasm. Perch on bathroom sink and smoke your first cigarette, one of David's Marlboro Reds. Feel, finally, like an adult.

- Use viewport to ID all visitors. A knock at the door could mean David's dad with a baseball bat. A knock at the door could mean the staff wants to clean the room, and you can't let them so close to David's pills. A knock at the door could mean that your mom convinced the man at the front desk to give her David's room number because you haven't come home, and your sister who can't lie told her you were here. Watch like a movie you can't pause as her headlights light up your naked body standing beside the 22-year-old whose heroin addiction you know she knows exists.
- Ensure that all windows and doors are locked. The door locks on its own. Worry anyway that some stranger—or, worse, your mother—will walk in and see you naked.

USE AND ABUSE

1. David and I are groping each other on Taylor's older sister's bed. My sisters crouch at its foot so their bodies won't block the light. Taylor surveys her scene. She's lined my eyes in thick kohl and put me in a black slip she cut so short my underwear shows if I move either leg even an inch. David wears what he always wears: white T-shirt, Levis. His feet are bare. I never see his feet bare. We are high on methadone and Xanax, barely aware of Beth and Chelsea or even Taylor. We act out our own little movie, everything black and white like the film in Taylor's camera. She'd asked us to pose for her, and I said we would because I wanted my friends to like my boyfriend, and I wanted the four-by-six-inch still images that would say *This really happened* in case David and I unravel like my slip threatens to do when he teases a thread. Taylor instructs David to kiss me: on the mouth, the neck. "Put your hands there," she says and points to my waist. She says, "Amy, move in closer. David, smile." David smiles. Taylor snorts out a laugh. "Not like that," she says. "Like a person." A genuine grin spreads across his face. Taylor snaps a photo. I'm so close to David I can feel the heat coming off his body and smell the tobacco and Old Spice that linger on his skin. I don't know what to do with my hands. Simulating sex we've never had feels like when people ask me what it's like to be a triplet, and I say, "I don't know what it's like to *not* be one." I'm still learning what people do in bed together. "Like this?" I ask. Taylor shrugs. "Just do what you usually do." I don't tell her that we don't really have a way we usually do things. David slips me a second

methadone pill. He takes two. Under the opioid euphoria, it's easy to pretend we really are just making out and not being photographed, that this moment is real instead of orchestrated. We don't forget Taylor's there, but we are good models. We do what she asks. We play ourselves: fucked up and infatuated.

2. David and I never had "the talk," that stuttering, awkward exchange between two people who aren't sure of their relation to each other or the words they should use to describe who they are together. We hung out a few times, and David was my boyfriend. It just happened. I think of it as happening the night he put his suede-and-sweater bomber jacket over my shoulders; I'd snorted a 2-milligram Xanax bar, and David held my waist so I wouldn't topple over on the walk back to my car from the Irish bar we'd had to leave. A bouncer asked to see my ID, and I was only eighteen. David downed his White Russian and took my hand, unconcerned. When I met him, David drank White Russians exclusively. He said they settled his stomach. And so my first drink was a White Russian, drunk at the duplex David rented in Niceville after his dad evicted him from the apartment above Tires Plus, a small chain of auto shops David claimed he'd inherit one day. The duplex is also where I got stoned for the first time. It was mostly a big living room off of which sprouted two bed-rooms and a cramped kitchen. I sat on the orange-plaid couch where David and I first kissed and drew tangy smoke into my lungs. I exhaled and receded into a tunnel. David went into his bedroom and ceased to exist. I heard his voice on the other side of the wall and couldn't stop laughing because I knew he wasn't really there. I don't think I've ever felt as free as I did then, all alone with only a drug for company.

3. Our modeling gig wrapped, David and I walk down Taylor's pebble-paved driveway to my car. I'm not wearing shoes, and the rocks jab at my feet. I'm

not wearing the slip anymore either, but I've kept it, balled in my denim tote. I tell David he should drive. He's on methadone all the time, and I've only done it twice; I figure he's more sober even though he's taken more. We're headed somewhere, but we don't make it. When David is high, he lists to the right. He does it walking, and he does it sitting up, and he does it driving cars, too. I notice he's drifting, but I think he'll correct his course. He's not that high. Is he? I start to say, "David, mailbox," and right then the airbags explode. The front of my car is a broken nose, a face punched so hard it's folded in on itself. Hardly even there. The trunk of a red-brick mailbox stands like ruins in the grass. David is yelling at the homeowner, accusing the man of having installed his mailbox too close to the road. I don't see their exchange. I'm scrambling into the driver's seat so it will look like I was always there when the police arrive. I can only see what's in front of me. Taylor drives past us with Beth and Chelsea in her passenger seats. They get out to help. One of my sisters calls the parents, and I get the same sinking feeling that guts me when a cop pulls me over for speeding or I tap someone's bumper in traffic. Like I could have turned back time if this hadn't happened, but now that it has time is steel-toed and irrevocable, solid as that brick, and I'm fucked. "A cat," I tell the mom in tears. "I saw it about to cross the road, and I tried to swerve, and then I tried to stop, and I turned the wheel the wrong way, or I was too close. I don't know. It happened really fast." I wonder if the mom can tell I'm high. I wonder whether she believes my story; it's not a stretch to think I'd sacrifice a car to save a cat. On the ride home, the mom doesn't ask if I'm high or lying or if David was driving. She says I need to calm down. I think Taylor takes David home, and I think Beth and Chelsea wait with the dad for the tow truck, but I don't know. All I see are flashing lights. I'm a wreck.

4. In Destin, all my friends hated David. They hated him because he was too

old for me and not good enough. They hated that he got me into drugs, and they hated seeing me on them. They hated watching David steal Barnes & Noble's magazines, which we read for free anyway in the adjoining mini-Starbucks. They hated how easily I let him fool me with purloined trinkets and bold but mostly empty declarations. They hated me, I think, the way I cleaved to David like he'd made me because he had. But, really, they hated him for being a junkie. I don't know how they knew except that everyone knew. You could hear the drugs in his voice; they flattened and stretched his vowels, rubberized his consonants. Leftover heroin reverberated under the methadone-and-Xanax slur that inflected his sentence structures and lazy pronunciations. He still says "him" like "eem" (rhymes with "beam"), omitting the hard "h" at the front and trading the *i* for an *e*. Drugs haunted the long pauses David took when he talked and filled with a sort of humming "Uhh" or "Ummm" or "I-I-I-I-I-I." You could see in the pinned pupils that sat like tiny periods at the center of his fat brown irises that David was high. Once, he came over to the house with Taylor and Ahmed. I'd warned him to stay quiet. "My parents won't think you're charming," I said. When I asked him not to mention drugs, he said "I'm not stupid." But you never knew what David might say. He poked his head into what we called the computer room to say a quick hello to the dad, who stood to shake David's hand, only half out of his chair, and returned to his online cribbage match. David rattled on to the mom about New York. He talked over her when she mentioned having visited the city for the 1964 World's Fair. Her story was more interesting, but to David his was more important; it established his credibility as a real person who'd done something other than hang around his hometown. I could see annoyance on the mom's face as David trailed her into the laundry room, her relief when the phone rang and she had an excuse to shoo him off. "He was nervous," I told the mom after David left. "Uh-huh," she said.

5. When Taylor developed the pictures, the people in them looked classic and cool like mid-century movie stars. David and I had known each other maybe a month, but here we appeared as a couple in love. Our eyes are glassy, our movements fluid. David's smile is sweet and sneaky like in real life; I appear eager and radiant, seasoned like I wanted David to think I was. We are lovers alone in bed, grunge glamorous and pre–car crash. We look so alive we might crawl over each other and out of the frame. Taylor gave me my copies, and I looked at them and forgot they were constructed. She'd always been good at candids. She kept the ones she took of all of us at the Waffle House and Walmart and on the picnic tables at school in fat photo albums that I flipped through when we hung out in her bedroom. I hid the slip and the pictures in a suitcase under my bed. I kept my writing there, and the mom knew not to look for it. Years later, I tore up my childhood bedroom in search of those photos. I wanted to see if they came out the way I remembered: dreamy and tender, David tough and golden and me tiny and smitten yet somehow powerful, a little slutty in the too-short slip and all that eyeliner. But I'd lost them; there are no copies in Taylor's albums, and she doesn't have the negatives. I found the slip, but I think the mom threw out the images of me in it when I was away at college and had told her David and I were done. Or it might have been me. I can imagine tossing them out in some attempt at cleansing when I still believed an *over* existed between David and me.

6. The mom cleans out the Intrepid while I'm at school. We have to take it to the dealership to see if it's totaled. It is. I spot it parked in the back of the lot, and I want to cry when I understand that not only have I lost my car but also everything that made it mine: the bulky phone beside the center console, all my mix tapes, the rat that Ahmed so meticulously cut off a PETA sticker

and attached to my bumper. (*Rats Have Rights Too!* the sticker proclaimed until Ahmed uncoupled the mascot from its message so the rat clawed at my license plate with skinny rat fingers that he said resembled my own.) But I can't tell anyone I'm sad about losing the car. The mom found one of David's empty Xanax bottles and paperwork from the methadone clinic in its glove compartment. The papers featured his actual age, his birthdate. "He's 22, and he's a heroin addict," the mom says while we await the mechanic's word. "What else do you need to know?" I can't look at her. The mom and I don't get into fights. "He's not a heroin addict," I say. "You don't know him. He's going to the methadone clinic. He wants to get better." The mom's face falls. "I don't even want you to know what a methadone clinic is."

7. David's mother loved me. I had seen his latest local ex, Kathleen, a hairdresser who wore product-crusted curls and too much makeup. She looked like the kind of woman men call "high maintenance." Her face was sharp, and her skin appeared lined and heavy despite or maybe because of the foundation she slathered all over it. I remember sitting in my car and watching David talk to her about money she owed him or money he owed her or the dog they'd shared, Nico, for whom David could never have provided proper care. David said they'd planned to get married. His mother must have been relieved he'd found a girl who wouldn't push her obviously vulnerable son into a legal union and ask for babies. She knew my parents a little. David's stepdad had coached Chelsea's softball team. She knew what kind of girl I was. If anything, she worried about what David might do to me. But, to David's dad, I was just another partner in crime. The day I met him, Mr. Mickelson showed us his young Japanese wife and sprawling suburban home and the miniature figurines he painted and displayed in a china cabinet until they sold on eBay. They were characters from *World of Warcraft* or something like it: princesses,

dragons, heroes with swords. The figurines were overtly sexual, and I felt awkward looking at them, nodding in faked admiration as David's dad handed me a porcelain figure barely larger than my thumb. I fidgeted with the woman warrior, big breasted and barely dressed, painted in soft, feminine purples and greens. I probably told him the pieces were impressive, and they were. All that detail on such a tiny canvas. But watching this man handle something that so resembled a child's toy felt obscene, perverted. David had told me about the way his father had treated him as a kid. David's dad was huge. Tall but mostly wide and fat so that in my head the scenes David described are grotesque flashes of big man belly pressed against little boy face, meaty massive man hand on little boy head, flabby man gut jiggling over little boy body, little boy David coiled inside his daddy's stomach like a fetus or a club sandwich. And David left me alone with him. I watched him boss around his wife, who winked at me as if to say, *Don't they all, though?* I fingered figurines to flatter a man who frightened me, whose presence lit in my chest an anger like crackling coal. I don't remember what we talked about or if we talked at all. I'd eaten too much Xanax or I've blacked it out, like taking a Sharpie to my brain. When David came back, he told me we needed to leave. I nodded and followed him out the door. We weren't gone five minutes before Mr. Mickelson called my car phone to demand back the $100 bill he knew David had taken from the stack he kept in his office. "Turn around here and stop for a second," David said. We buried the bill in a flowerbed at the entrance to his dad's neighborhood and drove back to the house. David's dad searched my car like a police detective and didn't find anything. David, a consummate liar, acted baffled, almost hurt, that his own father would suspect him of theft. The next night, Mr. Mickelson drove the 45 minutes from Milton to Destin with a baseball bat in his passenger seat. He stood inside the Tires Plus apartment, bat at his waist. His fist slid up and down the shaft. He called me a cunt and spit at his son a slew of names David had probably heard before. He wanted his money, but there was nothing to give. David had spent all of it on two overpriced oxys the night we'd retrieved the $100 from the flowerbed. Now he had to find a new place to live.

8. I'm not allowed to see David anymore after he crashes my car. The mom forbids it. The dad makes a rare trip up the stairs to yell at me. He looks ridiculous and incongruous on the window seat in my bedroom, a pink baby pillow at his back. He's nearly crushing Pretty Dog, the love-worn stuffed sheepdog I dragged with me everywhere as a child. And I feel ridiculous and incongruous, too, the dad unleashing on me an unhinged rant about the drug addict I'm dating amid all these artifacts of my girlhood. "It's like you go out of your way to date losers," he fumes. "I mean, that or you're just stupid." But I'm not stupid, and despite my tears, I'm not sad; I'm indignant. "If you raised me well," I say, "you should trust me to make my own decisions." The dad sneers. "If you made better ones, maybe I would." During my last few months in high school, it feels like all the dad ever does is yell at me. He doesn't know how to express love or its attendant fear appropriately; he uses money and bellicose monologues. To apologize for screaming at me, he buys me a brand-new Volkswagen Jetta, charcoal gray with matching leather interior. "But I crashed the Intrepid," I say as he leads me toward the new cars at his friend's dealership. "I shouldn't get a new car." I mean I don't deserve one. The dad thinks I'm not dating David anymore. "Once you've had a new car, you'll never want a used one again," he says, almost in code, like he's talking about men, too. But the dad never talks to me about men unless to express his dislike of the one I'm dating. The dealership doesn't have the gray exterior I like with the leather upholstery on which the dad insists, so I'm sent home in a white rental with cloth seats. I drive it straight to Tires Plus. David and I have plans.

"You can't smoke in a rental car," I say as he reaches into his jacket pocket for his Marlboros. "They won't notice," David says and lights up anyway.

9. When I came home smelling of cigarette smoke, the mom knew I'd been with David. I had lies. I'd say I'd been with Emily or Taylor; they smoked. I'd say I'd been with Ahmed and Tim at the Waffle House, where you could still smoke inside; we all left there smelling like a pool-hall floor. I had rituals I believed would protect me from detection. I kept a sock full of coffee grounds under my driver's seat because I'd read that coffee absorbed the smoke smell. I'd stop at gas stations and scrub my arms like a surgeon, run cheap pink soap through my hair. I bought Febreze and tied to my rearview mirror sticks of incense from the Zoo Gallery. Once, I told the mom I'd been in a thrift store. "Thrift stores don't smell like smoke," she said. She was sitting on the dark-wood bench inside our foyer, arms folded and body taut against its green velvet cushions. "No, but they're musty," I said. I stuck with my lies. I performed my rituals. But something or someone always betrayed me. A cigarette burn in my car's upholstery. Ashes on the steering wheel. The testimony of my sister who refused to lie for me. When she wanted to know where I was, the mom went to Beth. Beth would say she didn't know until she could no longer deflect the question. "Is she with that guy?" the mom asked one night. Beth squirmed in her seat. "I don't want to say," she said. "So, she is?" said the mom. Beth spilled the whole thing. "She's in Niceville. They're at Tisa's." I can imagine exactly how Beth would have said this: eyes down, mouth twitching as though the mom were pulling at the right side and I the left, her words barreling into each other like six cars in a pileup. She didn't want to tell on me, but she didn't want to tell the story I'd asked her to use on anyone who inquired after my whereabouts. The story did not involve telling the mom that I was at Tisa's, the motel where David lived then. Tisa's, now shuttered, was the kind of place

populated by what Joan Didion calls "motel people": drunks, junkies, day laborers, the working poor who can't pay first and last month's rent plus a security deposit all at once. The mom sped over the Mid-Bay Bridge and toward Valparaiso. Her headlights bounced as she pulled into the big Tisa's parking lot. I watched her enter the front office and ask a clerk for David Mickelson's room number. The man said he wasn't allowed to give out that information. "Well, my teenage daughter is in there with a 22-year-old man," the mom said. "I can call the police instead." The manager gave her the room number. I was caught. I couldn't lie about being with David when the mom could see him watching at the window as I climbed into her car. I apologized and teared up and, for the hundred-thousandth time, accused the mom of distrusting me. I reminded her that in a few months I'd be at college, and wouldn't she rather I make these mistakes now, when she could oversee them? "Get in the car," the mom said through gritted teeth. I sat in the passenger seat. She waved her hand in front of her face. "You smell like an ashtray," she said.

10. For a long time I refuse the cigarettes David offers me. I know I'll like smoking. I'll like it so much that I'll keep doing it, and I'll have to hide my habit from my family for the rest of my life. I cried when I caught the mom smoking by the side of the house in sixth grade, and the dad quit on Father's Day 1990-something, as if to guilt his daughters out of starting. He can tell you to the day when he smoked his last cigarette. By the time I smoke my first, it's warm outside, maybe March or April. I've ducked out of my three-hour painting class and snuck over to David's motel room in the middle of the day. He ushers me inside and kisses me hard like we haven't seen each other in weeks. He tastes like cigarettes and sleep. His hair is rumpled. The afternoon sun snakes through the fat-slatted plastic blinds, lending the room a neon cast. All the lights are off. I don't ask if David is high. "Come lay down," he

says. He's unbuttoning his pants. I make him turn around while I take off my clothes and crawl under the sheet. He's not allowed to look even when we're both naked in bed, legs touching legs, hips against hips, calves over thighs. I let him roam his fingers over my bare skin, and I'm not afraid because David never pressures me. Methadone decreases his libido, so he doesn't mind that I'm afraid to touch him. He taunts me to amuse himself. "I'll touch you with it," he says, dick in hand, and I squeal and wriggle out of his arms. I do want to touch his penis, and I don't. Touching a man's penis will mark a turning point for me, and I'm not sure I want to take the turn, or I want to take it slowly. Not because I want to savor the feel of the curve or because I like teasing this person who's so patient with me. I tease because I don't know what I'm turning into or where starting down that road might lead.

11. Everyone told me I was wrong. Had my friends not been so dismissive of my feelings, the mom so decisive in her edicts, the dad so cruel in his asser-tions about my relationships and what they said about me, I probably would have broken up with David of my own volition. Instead, I dug in my heels, determined to prove myself right. I could date a drug addict. I could make David a better person. David *was* a better person, more than what the chem-icals he ingested suggested about him. My friends and family just couldn't see what I saw. They hadn't confided in David and watched him really listen instead of treating their anxiety as a joke the way my parents and sisters and even my best friends did. No one else saw how cute and playful he was, chas-ing me up the Forest Ranger lookout tower to watch the sun set. They didn't know how often his mother walked in on him so overdosed his face had turned blue. They didn't sit up at night clutching their flip phones, convinced David was dead because he hadn't called when he said he would. They couldn't see how precarious David was and thus how precious.

12. At Tisa's, I duck my head under the covers to really look at David's naked body. I nuzzle my head into his chest like his penis is a scene in a horror movie I can't watch. When I graze it with my fingertips, the skin is dry and satin smooth, not at all the gummy-slime texture I'd expected since the time I walked in on the dad asleep and saw his dick peeking out of the seam of his boxer shorts like a miniature version of the giant worms in *Dune*. I jump back and approach again, touching David with hands like paws. I cradle his penis in my palm, and he lets out a little moan. "You can go harder," he says. I shake my head. "I don't know what I'm doing," I say, my voice like a little girl's. "I don't want to hurt you." David tells me I won't hurt him, and I don't need to know what I'm doing. "Just do what you think would feel good," he says. So I hold it, this thing made hard with blood and protruding from between my boyfriend's legs. He tells me to make a fist around it and squeeze. "Are you sure?" I ask. "It won't hurt," David promises again. "You're okay." I shake my head. I'm proud of my progress—actually interacting with the penis—but I'm also embarrassed and a little sad. The feelings drift through me the way a storm rolls onto land from over the Gulf of Mexico. "I don't want to," I tell him. David's hand is in my hair. His lips press against the top of my head. "Let me go down on you, then," he says. He's been saying it for days, weeks maybe. He says he likes doing it, and I can tell he likes telling me so. But what if there's something wrong with me down there? What if David puts his face in my vagina and finds it lacking in some way I won't recognize because the only vagina I know is my own, and I don't even know it well. I haven't touched it since I was a little kid, obsessed then with the velvet feel of its folds. I tell David he can touch me instead. Just on the outside. I don't know the words *vulva* and *labia*—or, I've heard them, but I don't know to which parts of me they refer. It's like the first time I got stoned. Only this bed

and David's hand and my shaking legs are real, as in really there. I close my eyes and see sweating pink skin like the skin inside me projected on a screen on the undersides of my eyelids. David asks again if he can go down on me, and his fingers feel so good I say yes. I've never done it before and so don't know what it means to come until I do. I'm pushing David away, saying, "It's too much," saying, "You have to stop," when he asks me if I felt myself finish. "I think so," I say. David places his hand on my pubic hair like he's petting it. "Did you feel, like, a rising kind of thing and then, like, a release?" he asks. I say I did, and I'm sure I did, but I'm making up my own definitions for words I ought to know: *rise* and *release, come.* David doesn't ask me to make him come. He watches me sprawl across the bed, my breath like a dog's pant and my hands rubbing my legs because I think it will make them stop quivering. David heads for the bathroom, and I get up to look for my panties. When he opens the door, I'm pulling my shirt over my head. Actually, it's the mom's Dolly Parton T-shirt from 1976. I'm newly enamored of my mother's things, and I like the incongruity of Dolly's signature on my flat chest, the pointing out of a lack. "Are you okay?" David asks. "Yeah," I say. "I just probably need to go." He walks to the bedside table and picks up his Marlboros. "Just stay for a cigarette." He holds one out to me, and I take it, let David light it for me. I don't even think about it. I don't think about the day the dad quit or how worried I was when I caught the mom smoking six years ago. I perch triumphant on the sink and exhale, that first-cigarette buzz clouding my brain, first-orgasm hum pulsing in my muscles. I don't just like smoking; I love smoking. I love it because I know I shouldn't smoke, because it makes my head swim, because it pulls me closer to David right when I feel closer to him than I've ever felt to a man. In my lungs I feel a power like the power in my orgasm, a power I don't understand and can't name but want anyway to wield myself someday. I don't know that I already do or how much pain growing into it will entail. I don't know it's what I'm arguing about in youth group or how fearsome and thus hated it is. I don't know that this power is, to most of the world, a weakness.

13. The first time David lied to me or maybe didn't, I was sitting on the brown-and-tan shag carpet in the Niceville duplex's living room. He sat in a chair beneath one of the room's two windows. David divided the room into two sides: a living room and a dining room. The living room side held the couch and a coffee table and a couple of chairs for guests. On the other side he'd either planned to or really did put a vintage kitchen table with a patterned Formica top and matching metal chairs cushioned in mustard-yellow vinyl. The image remains so vivid in my memory that I can't decide whether I made up the table or it actually existed. We'd just been to visit dogs at the Humane Society. David was telling me about the chihuahua he and Kathleen shared when they lived together, how he missed little Nico and wanted her back. And then he moved to the floor, took my hands in his. "I have to tell you something," he said. I knew from the timbre of his voice that it was something serious, but I didn't think that what David needed to say would have anything to do with me. I thought it was drugs. Money. Maybe even something good: an achievement, a compliment, a gift. When he said, "I had sex with Kathleen," I pulled my hands out of his lap and turned away so he wouldn't see me cry. It was the first time he'd hurt me. "I'm sorry," he said. "It was a couple of months ago. I didn't think—I mean, we don't have sex." I turned to look at him. "That's your excuse? *We don't have sex?* How am I supposed to take that?" David reached for my hands again, and I let him take them because, now that I was angry, I could look him in the eye. He said he meant it didn't count as cheating since it wasn't something we'd ever done together. He just missed sex, he said. He hadn't done it to hurt me. He would never hurt me. "I don't believe this,"

I said. My last boyfriend had dumped me because he'd made out with another girl, and now this boyfriend, the boyfriend who was supposed to restore my faith in boyfriends, was telling me he'd fucked someone else, and it was my fault for being a frigid prude. I shook my head and said again, "I don't fucking believe this." "Good," David said. "Because I didn't do it." I could never tell when David was lying because his eyes were so sedate, his voice so monotone unless he wanted something I could give him. "I'm fucking with you," he said and squeezed my hands, swaying them right to left as if his palms were inviting mine to waltz. "I swear. I would never do that to you. I love you." *I love you* was how David got out of everything. Because he loved me, I was supposed to forgive whatever he said or did. "How am I supposed to trust you now?" I asked. I got up and paced the room. David promised he'd been lying. He said he wanted to see how I'd react, and he was sorry for upsetting me. He'd made a mistake. I didn't want to lose this person I'd grown to love during my hard and stupid fight to keep him. I nodded. "Okay," I said and swallowed my tears. Twelve years later, I know that David did and did not cheat on me. He says now that he went over to Kathleen's, that he was going to fuck her, but when they moved upstairs to her bed he felt so guilty he couldn't get hard. Back then, I didn't know what to believe, so I decided to believe he hadn't done anything. If I was wrong and he'd really cheated, it didn't matter. He was still there. He still wanted me.

14. I'm half dressed in the Jetta's backseat, my body wrapped around David, who's unbuttoning his pants. After I get over the hurdle of our bodies, they're almost never separate. I run to Tisa's any chance I get, or David meets me in Destin. The security guards who patrol the Silver Sands Outlet Mall catch us fucking around on a golf cart we found abandoned behind the Ralph Lauren store. Now, we're parked in the back of the Publix lot. David is trying to

convince me to let him attend my high-school graduation. "I'll stand in the back," he says. "I won't even talk to you." My whole family is coming to watch my sisters and me receive our diplomas: aunts and grandparents and a baby cousin. "Someone will see you," I say. "It's boring anyway. I don't even want to go. Why would you sit through a hundred names just so you can see me walk across a stage for 30 seconds?" David thinks I should risk estranging myself from my whole family because I love him. I think we'd be smarter to stay away from each other over the summer so that, by fall, everyone will think we've really, finally broken up. "Do you still want me to move to Gainesville?" he asks. We've been saying that David will move to Gainesville as soon as he can raise the money, after I settle into the dorm room I'll barely occupy at the University of Florida. If I say yes this time, I can't take it back. It's just that I'm not so sure anymore. I'm so unsure about so many things, and if I lug David and all his baggage to Gainesville, I'll also bring this uncertainty. I'll always wonder what would have happened if I'd said no. I'm thinking I'll tell him I'd rather he stay here, that we can decide later. But David's sitting right there. I can't control my facial expressions. He'll read between my frown lines and know what I want to say. I don't even consider that maybe David doesn't care. Maybe I'm his excuse to get out of the Panhandle, which reels people in and hooks them like the caught swordfish on the sign that greets drivers who enter Destin ("The World's Luckiest Little Fishing Village") from Oka-loosa Island, a strip of land where the Choctawhatchee Bay meets the Gulf of Mexico. It doesn't occur to me that, really, I'm more like that swordfish and David the hook tugging at my smiling mouth while the fish who weren't stupid enough to take the bait swim untethered below me like a hundred little possibilities. I've changed so much with David that I don't know anymore who I am alone, and don't I deserve the chance to figure it out? But I can't take it without hurting him. "Of course I want you there," I say. "I love you."

15. When David said he loved me, he didn't just say "I love you." He said, "I love you more than anybody ever has or ever will." He told me he wanted to build us a modest house with a white picket fence and fill it with babies. "But I don't like babies," I'd say. "Cats, then," David said. We would have cats, and I would write, and David would get a job working on cars, and he'd always love me more than anyone else because he'd be the only one I gave the chance. When he declared his love this way, it scared me. What if David really was it? What if I never had another boyfriend? It's why I decided not to have penetrative sex with him. I wanted something to remain new to me so I could look forward to sharing it with someone who hadn't been the first to look at and really see me. After we broke up, I started to think of David's declaration as a threat. When he said, "I love you more than anybody ever will," he was telling me that, if we broke up (and of course we'd break up; I knew before he moved to Gainesville that one day we would break up), I'd never find real love again. He was saying *You're unloveable to everyone but me.* I don't think he meant to suggest that only he saw anything worth loving in me, or he didn't mean it consciously. But that implicit message was supposed to intimidate me, to make me cling to him more desperately than I already did. David didn't know how to love me without manipulating me, and I didn't know enough about love to know that he was. Most of the things I think I know about love I learned from the time I spent with David. In the dozen years since we broke up, no one has loved me the way David did. I don't mean that no one else has loved me and also treated me like shit or that love never again revealed layers of myself I hadn't previously seen. I mean that since I left David and went back to David and left David again, I've remained basically alone. I haven't called anyone my boyfriend since I was nineteen. When I think about the way David used to declare his love, what scares me most is that time will prove him right.

GAINESVILLE MOTOR LODGE: INSTRUCTIONS & SECURITY

INSTRUCTIONS

1. Fully insert keycard. Hope custodial staff heeded the "Do Not Disturb" sign you hang on the door every time you leave. If they didn't, they've seen the empty coke bags and remnants of snorted pills on the TV cabinet. If they didn't, they'd probably have kicked you out by now.

2. Remove keycard. The keycard reminds you of the cards you use to get into your dorm room, which acts more like a storage facility now. You do most of your living in this motel room because David can't afford to rent a real apartment. David can't afford his own prescriptions or the coke you snort together. Pay for the prescriptions. Pay for the coke. Suppress your anger over all the money you spend on David. He's on the other side of the door.

3. Depress handle and open door. Depress yourself when you enter the room and see evidence of your drug use, clothes at the foot of the bed, overflowing ashtrays, empty cigarette packs, CVS bags that once contained David's prescription bottles. You can ignore the mess when you're high, but right now you're not. You're sober, coming home from class. Depress yourself again. You just called a motel room *home*.

FOR YOUR SECURITY

- Keep all pills on your person because you don't know whether motel employees can access the safe. Don't worry about police. You and David are white and clean, and you have a college ID.

- Secure deadbolt. Curse deadbolt when David locks you out during a fight and leaves you stranded on the highway-facing skywalk in panties and a threadbare T-shirt in the middle of the night. Bang on door. But, wait, not too loud. Someone might hear and then see you. Crouch and plead. Wait. Bang again with moderated fists. Wait. When he lets you back inside, cry on David's shoulder. Tell him how scared you were so he can insist you knew he only meant to tease you. It was three minutes. Of course he'd never leave you out there all night. Don't you know that?

- Use viewport to ID all visitors. A knock at the door could mean a cop. A knock at the door could mean a maid or the motel's management. A knock at the door could mean some other junkie who knows where you live and wants your money or David's pills. A knock at the door could mean David's mom, who pays for the room. A knock at the door could mean your own mother, who would kill you if she knew you'd eschewed the dorm room for which your dad pays to live in this motel with that drug addict they both told you to quit seeing.

- Keep your keycard on you at all times. If you lose it, you'll have to ask the night clerk to open your door, and he'll see what you and David have been doing in this room that isn't really yours.

- Ensure that all windows and doors are locked. The single door locks automatically, so you don't need to worry about the door. Worry about it anyway. Worry about it outside at night in your underwear while you knock and jiggle the handle and try not to scream. If you scream, that someone you're scared will come out to gawk at your bare legs could instead decide to call 911 or walk over and intervene; that someone might try to fix it. Refuse all belief in fixing it. If no one hears you, no one will see how cruelly David can treat you or that you let him and love him anyway, that you believe him when he says he loves you, too.

Duane Reade
328 Pearl Street
New York, NY 10038
(212) 385-0421

The pharmacist won't tell you over the phone if she has in stock the controlled substance you need. The pharmacist won't tell you anything about controlled substances unless you're inside the pharmacy, prescription in hand. Paul says the pharmacist thinks you're calling from a payphone down the street, that you'll signal to your boyfriend, who will enter the pharmacy with a note and a pistol and rob it. But you don't have a boyfriend or a gun. You're not going to rob the pharmacy. You have a prescription for 200 30-milligram oxycodone pills and don't want to run all over Manhattan with a migraine looking for them. But you do have to run all over Manhattan, head pulsing like a rabbit heart, because the pharmacist won't tell you whether she has your pills or if another store has them or if any Duane Reades have any oxys at all. Start where you always do, at the Pearl Street Duane Reade. You can see it from your bosses' office windows. You're pretty sure the Pearl Street Duane Reade doesn't even stock C-IIs, but test it anyway. Imagine how different—how tranquil, how balanced—a life you could lead if your oxys were only a step across the street, as accessible to you as are antibiotics and insulin and birth control pills to their consumers. The pharmacist here is a young guy, blond and bland as a Saltine cracker. "Do you have... this?" you ask in pharmacy voice. Pharmacy voice sounds like hurt. Pharmacy voice amplifies the pain you modulate your everyday voice to conceal. Step on that effects pedal in your throat and distort it. Add in some reverb, a little quiver on the last syllable. The pharmacist at the Pearl Street Duane Reade leans in to listen. He gives your script a glance and asks someone something you can't hear. He shakes his head. "We don't stock that medication," he says. He looks a little apologetic, but mostly he looks at you like all the pharmacists look at you. He looks at you like you're a junkie. Nod and knead your temples with your index fingers. Ignore the judgment in his eyes and say, "Thanks." Pharmacy voice on a feedback loop. Pharmacy voice obscures how much you'd rather punch the pharmacist on his smug little mouth than listen to him tell you that he can't tell you which drugs which Duane Reades keep on their shelves. You're no longer a voice on the phone—you're a 27-year-old woman, underweight and wearing sunglasses inside and rubbing the tender spots on the top of her head, clutching a legitimate prescription—but you're still a suspect. Walk out angry and a little more hopeless despite having known when you walked in exactly how the scene would play.

CVS Pharmacy-Photo
132 Front Street
New York, NY 10038
(212) 233-5134

Next, check the CVS across from the Front Street subway station. Its pharmacist, a middle-aged black man who wears a white knit kufi cap, dons an
exasperated expression like he can't believe you've dared enter a nationwide
pharmacy chain to ask for a drug. Be careful. Hold tight to the blue paper
Paul gave you. This same pharmacist once took your prescription and refused
to give it back. He said it looked suspicious. Your prescriptions are always
suspicious because you're young and able-bodied and getting an awful lot of
the instant-release oxy 30s that junkies covet. In the Front Street CVS, everyone looks suspicious. Everyone looks like they live in Yonkers or New Jersey.
There is a PATH train on this street, but there are PATH trains on lots of
streets, and those places don't feel like portals to 1999. Join the drab, defeated
people in scrunchies and elastic-waisted jeans on line at the pharmacy counter, beside a scuffed-up display that doesn't make sense because aren't all CVS
displays the same, and doesn't the one at 14th Street look clean and even a bit
glamorous? The Front Street CVS is crowded and dirty and weighed down
by a sense of gritty resignation that seeps into you while you wait. You've

never actually filled a prescription here, but you came close one time. You couldn't find your pills anywhere but at this CVS, which had 60 of them. You asked the pharmacist again and again to grant you an IOU or to hold onto the 60 pills so that you could try University Chemists before you gave up two-thirds of that month's prescription in exchange for a six-day supply. While you waited for his final refusal, a scraggly, heavyset blonde offered to meet you in the morning and spit some of her methadone into your mouth. She scrawled her phone number into your Moleskine, and you knew you had to find oxys somewhere and fast. If you didn't, you might actually call her. In the hour you spent traveling to and from the Lower East Side, someone else took CVS's 60 oxys. You didn't have enough pills to make it through the next day, let alone the week that could pass before the pharmacies restocked their opioids, so Paul wrote you a temporary supply of Dilaudid. Since then, the pharmacist at the Front Street CVS says, "We're out," every time you bring in a prescription. You swear there's something he doesn't like about you, some reason he doesn't think you deserve pain relief. But you have to try. Everybody takes a day off sometime.

Duane Reade
10 Irving Place
New York, NY 10003
(646) 602-2583

Get on the train at Fulton Street and head to Union Square. Paul has admitting privileges at a hospital near the Irving Place Duane Reade. He tried to convince them to let you use the actual hospital pharmacy, but the actual hospital pharmacy is for actual hospital patients. Sometimes you imagine getting yourself admitted to the hospital just so you can use its pharmacy. You imagine shelves and shelves of narcotics just upstairs, shelves and shelves of pain relief stretching out of your grasp like something from *Alice in Wonderland*. But there's a pain management practice in the huge glass building that houses the hospital, so the miniature Duane Reade you're allowed to patronize stocks painkillers to service its patients. If it services you, shove the crinkly white bag into the bottom of your purse and clench your fist around the oversized leather bag's beat-up straps. Your full prescription is worth anywhere from $3,500 to $9,000 on the black market. Someone might kill you for that. But more and more often, the Irving Plaza Duane Reade tells you they're out, too. You're not sure if the pharmacists are lying or if you're missing the pills, whether you'd leave with a filled script if only you could make it there a few minutes sooner. Most of the people you see in the Irving Place Duane Reade look like pain patients: elderly and in wheelchairs, wearing casts on their arms, walking with canes. You are ruthless. You shoot through the lobby, darting past a decrepit old man so that you'll make it first to the pills you know he's gunning for, too. Let yourself feel bad when you hear the man asking the pharmacy techs where he can get his prescription filled—he doesn't know the geopolitics of it all—but you can't dwell on his problem. You are just like him, only younger and faster and nastier. And he doesn't look like a doctor shopper or a drug seeker the way you do. The pharmacist doesn't assume that patients with leg braces or walkers or full heads of gray hair just want to get high. At Irving Place, the pharmacist is a Chinese American woman shaped like an apple. She's flanked by two young techs: a girl who pulls her sandy-brown hair into a tight ponytail and a good-looking black guy with impeccably tattooed forearms. The guy fills your script without giving you shit, but the girl always has the pharmacist's back. Once, she called over the pharmacist to ask whether your doctor's signature looked a little different than usual. "His signature always looks a little different," you said. "Pull up his signatures. Look. They're all a little different." The pharmacist called Paul's office anyway. The practice had closed almost two hours earlier, and she made you wait while his answering service paged him. The pharmacist got Paul on the phone and honored your prescription, but she also clucked her tongue and claimed that your doctor was "none too happy with you." Her words devastated you. You trust Paul. The two of you sign off on emails with *Love*. He shows you his crocheting projects and pictures of his curly-haired dog Teddy. He uses himself as an example when he needs to convince you that no drug is as scary as you think it is. When you were afraid to try Prozac, Paul said, "I'm probably being unprofessional here," and described the depression that haunted him after his parents' sudden deaths. "It didn't make me a different person," he told you, "but it cleared the fog." He said that, without the Prozac, he wouldn't be your doctor. He wouldn't be anyone's doctor because he wouldn't have made it through medical school, and he might be dead. "But I'm a sample size of one," he reminded you, and he let you take your time deciding whether you wanted to try SSRIs. You get that you're not an easy patient, but Paul likes a challenge, and you are like a puzzle whose pieces never quite fit together. He's always saying, "I wish I could do more for you," as if he doesn't know he's doing everything. After you got your script filled by the Duane Reade tech with the cheerleader ponytail, you emailed to let Paul know you had your pills and apologized for causing him stress. You told him what the pharmacist said and that you were sorry for whatever you'd done to upset him. *I hope you know I would tell you myself if I were mad at you,* Paul replied in an email late that night. He said he'd been frustrated with the pharmacist. *If just once they'd call to tell me about a drug interaction I missed or ask me about a cheaper generic I could have prescribed, I wouldn't mind so much, but it's always some petty thing that makes you stressed out and me angry.* He started switching you back and forth between 20- and 30-milligram oxys so that you could get new pills before the requisite 27 days had passed. Now, he lets you pick up your prescriptions a week early so that, when you go to fill them, every pharmacist's shaking head won't send you spinning into crisis mode.

Walgreens
485 8th Ave
New York, NY 10003
(212) 677-0327

You're never able to stop yourself from dropping in on the Walgreens at 14th and 8th when the Irving Place Duane Reade fails you. Walgreens is right across the street, and even though it always fails you, too, you're sure that the day you skip this Walgreens will end up the only day in the store's history on which it stocks oxycodone. Its aisles are narrow and its shelves low; you can stretch your neck and see the toothpaste stacked opposite the hair dye. Hurry to the pharmacy counter in the back of the store. It's desolate there, as though the pharmacy holds nothing at all and so everyone knows to avoid it. Show your prescription to the pharmacist, a kind 50-something white man with a salt-and-pepper crewcut and ask if he can fill it because you never know. Except you do. He can't. Your pulse ticks off the minutes you've wasted. You feel stupid for even bothering. But it's too tempting: a pharmacy, right there at the corner of hope and your breaking point.

Duane Reade
142 Greene Street
New York, NY 10012
(646) 613-9042

The Duane Reade across from Washington Square Park must at least sometimes have your pills. The store is huge. The store is its own city block. The pharmacy counter is long and clean and as tall as you are. Behind it sit rows of medications in white boxes. That a cache of oxycodone isn't hiding among them seems impossible. The absurdity of the absence would amuse you if you didn't need the pills so badly. Stand on the tips of your toes so the pharmacist can see you. She's one of those women whose age you can't guess because she's probably looked the way she looks now since she turned 25 and won't age again until she hits her 60s. She is as angular as the counter, her spine straight and her brown hair pulled back in a slick bun. She looks as if she would pair red-heeled stilettos with her white coat. Her speaking voice is small and quiet as a librarian's, but her verdict is firm. "No, we don't," she says when you ask her if they've got 30-milligram oxys. You keep your prescription in sight so she knows why you're asking, but when you left the Irving Place Duane Reade, you quit caring about the judging pharmacists and began panicking about whether you'd ever procure your pills. The pharmacist consults a computer for a long time. She consults the shelves. She goes back to her computer. "We might get it on Wednesday," she says. By Wednesday, you'll be in withdrawal. "Sorry." She says it in the tone you use when people ask you questions on the subway and you just want to read your book undisturbed. Sometimes you skip this Duane Reade. It's too sad, and it compounds your pessimism. Not because they don't have your painkillers. You never expected them to have your painkillers. You're just checking because you have to check everywhere. You're checking in case by some fluke in the supply chain they got Irving Place's stuff. This Duane Reade is sad because it feels abandoned. The pharmacist looks so bitter and lonely that you almost feel sorry for her. But don't make a habit of feeling sorry for pharmacists. For all you know, she's sitting on the oxycodone, waiting for you to leave so she can laugh with her tech about the desperate addict she turned away. Picture it, how she'd stick her pointed chin in the air and say, "We'll never be like that hole-in-the-wall Irving Place branch."

Metro Drugs
891 Park Avenue
New York, NY 10065
(212) 794-7306

You used to go north if you couldn't find your pills at the Irving Place Duane Reade, but now you don't even bother with pharmacies above 34th Street. They never have anything. During one especially frustrating refill attempt, you tried a Metro Drugs on the Upper East Side. You picked up the habit of looking in people's medicine cabinets from David, so you know that rich people usually keep at least one narcotic prescription in theirs. Surely, you thought, pharmacies in more affluent neighborhoods kept themselves better stocked than their downtown counterparts. Where else would New York's elite get those bottles filled with Vicodin and Xanax? But your assumption proved incorrect. Or maybe the pharmacists noted your Brooklyn address and didn't want to risk giving a controlled substance to outer-borough riff-raff. Perhaps they asked themselves what you were doing so far from your doctor's office, which is just north of Houston. They might have deemed you a pharmacy hopper, decided you had to go all the way up to 68th and Park because the NoHo pharmacists had red-flagged you. Pharmacists lie all the time. They call it "using their discretion."

University Chemists
74 University Place
New York, NY 10003
(212) 473-0277

You'll find out about University Chemists after the pharmacy situation gets so bad that Paul starts making Allen, his office manager, call pharmacies for you. Pharmacists admit to medical personnel things they would never tell a patient. Allen looks for pain management clinics and calls the pharmacies that fill their prescriptions. University Chemists is an independent pharmacy, which means both that it operates under more empathetic guidelines than a chain pharmacy and that no one there knows whether you filled a month's supply at Duane Reade three or 30 days ago. The pharmacist, an older man of Middle Eastern descent, will give you all the oxys he has, and if what he has doesn't cover your full prescription, he lets you come back and collect the rest when he gets a new shipment. He keeps track in his head of when his patients will next need their meds; if no one else needs what you need that day, he'll hold your pills until you make it there to pick them up. If he doesn't have your pills, he'll point you in the direction of pharmacies that probably do even if it means losing your business that month. Sometimes he'll call around for you. He understands the way pain patients catastrophize. He sees how hard it is, all the stomping around sidewalks and stepping over red tape. Walking into University Chemists feels like entering someone's home. University Chemists doesn't look like a home. It looks like a pharmacy built in the 1980s and never fully updated. It doesn't have a computer or a self-swipe credit-card machine or even a waiting area. You reach over a low counter to hand your prescription to the pharmacist. You wait on a folding chair by a tiny rack of greeting cards or wander the aisles that hold only essentials: vitamins and NSAIDs, feminine hygiene products and diapers, deodorant and soap. There's no refrigerator full of ice cream sandwiches and microwave pizzas or entire row dedicated to pet supplies. No table fans or magazines. No bright overhead lights or ultra-clean lines or chest-high counter so the pharmacist looks down on you like a judge looking down on a defendant. Once you learn about University Chemists, make it your first stop, or wait until Allen calls to say he found your oxys there. Put down the phone and tell your boss you'll be back in half an hour; a pharmacy has your pills, and you can't risk letting them go to someone else. Hop on the 5 train or the A, limbs quivering with animal fear. Even though Allen promises that University Chemists can fill your script, you aren't safe until the pharmacist says, "Do you want to wait on it?" You always want to wait on it. Sit in the folding chair and try to concentrate on your book until he hands you the bag. Wrap your hand around the bottle to confirm it's there. Walk back to the subway nearly out of your body. Leaving a pharmacy with painkillers in your purse is like surviving a car accident sans seatbelt. You're grateful, relieved, and—for just a second—invincible. But it doesn't last. The cycle restarts the minute you're back in your cubicle, always late because you exit out the wrong side of the subway and don't know where you are. You are here. Collect 200 pills and two weeks of peace. Land on Pearl Street. Repeat. Repeat. Repeat.

COMEDOWN

1. I ask my therapist if I'm too old to not know I'm bipolar. "Not necessarily," Nancy says. I'm settling onto her couch. I take off my scarf and my coat and put my gloves inside my hat. "Have you ever taken a mood stabilizer?" she asks. I shake my head, and the ache in it stabs me in the side of my skull. "Or, no. I took Seroquel once in college when a dealer ripped off my friend," I say and explain how Brian knew he wasn't being handed the painkillers we'd asked for but decided to take the big white pills anyway. The guy already had our money. We Googled the imprint, read about the drug, and ate one each just to see what an antipsychotic would do to us. I heard voices and fell asleep for thirteen hours. Brian took his right before he took a six-hour drive from Gainesville to our hometown in the Florida Panhandle. He had to pull over on the side of the road because the trees were dancing. He told me they looked like those balloon men with the extra-long arms. But I don't know if an antipsychotic is at all similar to a mood stabilizer, and I can't listen to Nancy explain how mood stabilizers work because what if I'm bipolar? I wanted my therapist to say that of course I'm not bipolar, that if I were I'd have exhibited symptoms before I turned 30. "How would I know if I needed a mood stabilizer?" I ask. Nancy draws a diagram on her whiteboard. Next to a line near the top, she writes *ceiling*. Another line represents the floor. She scrawls squiggly waves that model the mood shifts I'd experience if I had each of the three major types of bipolar disorder. The third type sounds

indistinguishable from depression to me: a long period just above the floor punctuated by intermittent attacks that lay the sufferer so low Nancy's marker hits the whiteboard's bottom edge. It looks like what I'd have drawn had she asked me to show her how I've felt over the past three weeks. I don't say that. Instead I say, "I don't know how much stability I want in my moods." Nancy shrugs like I've made a valid point.

2. The mom thinks the opioids I take for my chronic headaches make me negative and depressive. Tom used to say I obsessed over them. "You want me to tell you it's okay to take another one, like you need me to sanction every pill," he said once, which isn't true. Tom thinks my headaches result from the way I relate to people, how I orient myself in the world. He says if I engaged differently with my pain, I wouldn't feel it; if I didn't obsess over how many pills I have, I wouldn't need them. He doesn't understand that I have to obsess. Pain management requires discipline. If I always took the amount I need to not have a headache, my prescription wouldn't last through the month. I'm accountable to the doctor who writes all 120 of the oxys I take per month now, and I have to think about whether another doctor will write the same quantity later. I'm not going to live in Southwest Virginia forever. I don't want to up my tolerance until I'm back to taking 300 milligrams every day. I'm obsessed with the calendar, the clock, and the calculator in ways I wouldn't be if I weren't taking a highly regulated narcotic that, at present, is better known for its addictive than analgesic properties. Most of the time, I have to decide which part of the day I can spend in pain. When I lived in New York, I rarely took more than one oxy over nine hours at work; it felt wasteful, using valuable painkillers when I'd feel hateful and miserable no matter how mild my headache. In my MFA program, I applied the same logic to teaching; whether I took one or two oxys when I woke up, the pain returned about fifteen minutes into my morning composition class, sickly and bulbous or

angular, stabbing; feverish or cooly brittle like a dry wind; and always pulsating, always tight, tense. Sometimes I decide to fuck it, take as many pills as I need to write all day or sleep or watch my Sunday premium-cable shows free of head pain. I can make it up later, take fewer on other days. Some months my regimen works, and others I spend the last week or two with an icepack pressed to my forehead, supplementing with judicious doses of Advil to placate headaches on which I can't expend narcotics or I'll come up short before I can fill my new script. I only have so many days to "make it up" before I run out.

3. I tell Nancy about the day before, when I called the Samaritans. Their website says you don't have to be suicidal to call, but the counselor didn't seem to know what to do with me. "That must be hard," he kept saying before he parroted back to me what I'd just told him. "It must be really hard to be in pain all the time" or "It must be hard doing all that alone." I asked him what the hotline was supposed to do for me. "I already know it's hard," I said. I try to describe to Nancy the way I'm crawling out of my skin at the same time that I'm burrowing further into it, but when I talk, it doesn't sound like enough. "I can't stop crying," I say. "I'm sad, and I'm angry, and I don't know why. I'm sick of everything. It's the end of winter break, and I'm still so tired." She asks me for specifics, examples. "I miss the routine," I say. "I want my life to have structure again. I don't have anything to do but write, but I don't have enough pills to write more than a few days a week, so what do I do on the other days? And then there's nothing on TV at night, and I hate reading in artificial light." Nancy asks me what I'll do when school starts that I don't do now. "That's the thing. Nothing, really," I say. "Or, no. I mean, I'll have the structure. It's easier to feel motivated when I have to plan what I want to do around what I have to do. Like, when getting to write feels special. But mostly I'm bored. I'm sick of myself. I want to see people more, and that won't get easier." Nancy knows I don't drink and that drinking is about the only thing my friends

here do; here, as in most college towns and most MFA programs, socializing is synonymous with drinking. To watch other people drink, even to spend a few hours talking with someone in my living room, requires an extra half painkiller, sometimes a whole one. "I'm alone too much, I guess," I say. I'm telling the truth, but none of what I tell Nancy describes what's bothering me specifically. Nothing is bothering me specifically. Everything bothers me. "I don't want to do anything; I don't want to think about anything. I don't want to get off the couch. But I'd like to get out of the house more. I'm in my head all the time. It's a shitty place. I wouldn't want to hang out with me." I pause. "I want to be a person who does things. I have a whole list of stuff I want to write. My brain won't turn off. I don't get how I can feel so overwhelmed and so fucking bored at the same time." I'm aware that I sound manic. I wonder if Nancy is assessing me for bipolar symptoms. "If I could write, I don't think I'd feel like this," I say. "But I don't have enough painkillers to write." Nancy says I should tell Audrey, my doctor in Blacksburg, exactly what I've told her. "You can't live like this," she says. I nod. I know.

4. I started writing again because I had headaches. I wrote all the time as a kid. I placed in some giant Scholastic contest my senior year in high school; only when a letter came in the mail did I remember I'd submitted a story. I made it exactly to the level at which I received a certificate and got my name on a list but did not have my story published. I was relieved. I didn't quit writing because I didn't think I was good; I quit because I couldn't invite people to see my insides. I was too scared to take creative writing classes as an undergraduate. I had never shown my work to anyone, and I didn't know if I wanted to share it with strangers when I had a grade at stake. And what the hell did I have to say? I told myself I was happy enough with academic writing or writing at work, and I thought I was. But in New York I couldn't stop crying. I hated my job, or I guess it was two jobs; neither nonprofit could afford a full-time employee, so they split me. I felt unappreciated

and overworked, like a sitcom character who books two dates for the same night, except everyone already knew I played two roles. I had one coworker who came in for four hours twice a week. I liked him, but it was lonely in my cubicle, and one of my bosses snapped at me for every mistake I made. The city noise, the subway cars and children's screams and all the sirens, crowded my head. I felt like the concrete and metal had gotten inside me somehow and were scraping pieces off my brain. But I was reading more than I had since I finished my first stint in grad school and left Gainesville for Santa Cruz. My commute gave me time and incentive. I'd missed all those words, their shapes and sounds. For the first time in eight years, I wrote something. I read it at a Brooklyn bookstore in front of maybe 50 people. The audience clapped in earnest. I almost won the bottle of wine awarded to the most-applauded reader, which I couldn't have drunk anyway. "You know that's your wine," I whispered to my friend Jen as she clapped for another writer. But I didn't care much whether anyone liked what I'd written. I didn't need to win. I needed to be a writer again.

5. Every fourth Thursday, I see Audrey, the PA who refills my painkillers. This Thursday, I get to her office an hour early. I keep my sunglasses on so the lights won't make my headache worse. I have cream-cheese-and-chive sandwich crackers in my purse in case I get hungry and Ben Lerner's second novel, *10:04*, to read. I keep trying to read it, but I don't feel like reading. I haven't felt like reading in almost a week. I've never not wanted to read. It's what made me think my symptoms were bipolar. I'm a third of the way through *10:04*. I want to finish it, but I don't want to read it. I like the book. I even feel a kinship with it. Lerner says he planned to write a story "involv[ing] a series of transpositions: I would shift my medical problem to another part of the body [and] change names." Of his planned next novel, he writes, "*Everything will be the same as it is now* [...], *just a little different.*" But Lerner couldn't get excited about transposing his experience

into fiction. He ended up writing a book about writing a book, about time and subjectivity and mortality. I spent a year trying to fictionalize my life, too. I'd have the me character meet David in college rather than high school. College could explain my character's motivations for dating him. I wrote two chapters, but getting my characters to do anything felt like moving clay figures through mud. When I decided to just write what happened, the whole thing opened up. So, I want to read the book. I would probably benefit from reading the book. But I'm just holding it while I fake a nap in the waiting room. The book makes me want to write, and I can't, so the book makes me want to cry, and I'm sick of doing even that.

6. I have this memory of myself crying in the shower; I must have been eleven or twelve. I'd stand under the running water and just fucking bawl. I didn't think anyone could hear me there. The mom came upstairs once to ask me what was wrong. "I don't know," I said. "I don't know." I felt wretched, and I had no idea why or what about. I don't think my crying shocked the mom. I'd always been a tightly wound child. But I don't think she knew what to do for me either. When I was seven, our pediatrician blamed my headaches on self-inflicted stress. No one ever suggested that I see a therapist or expressed concern that a child put so much pressure on herself. My parents didn't fight; they never beat or neglected me. I did well in school. I had friends. There was food on the table. There was always a table and a roof under which to put it. I had no apparent reason to worry the way I did. I want to know what I was worried about, why my brain works this way. I want to know what might have happened to my headaches—to me—if I'd had the opportunity to articulate what I felt to someone who knew how to deal with it before it lodged in my brain like a city's worth of concrete.

7. I'm nervous when the nurse calls me into the back. I put my purse and jacket on a chair so that she can weigh me (I'm at 106.4 this time; I fluctuate with each

visit). We go into a room filled mostly by an exam table, white paper smoothed over its leather upholstery. I sit on it while I have my blood pressure taken—the nurse gives me the numbers, but they don't mean anything to me—and answer a few questions. When the nurse leaves, I move into a black leather chair that looks like the moon waxing gibbous. I give up on *10:04* and examine the photocopied records I picked up from the Blacksburg Center for Pain Management before Dr. Piven closed his practice. Piven's notes sum me up in 100-word paragraphs. He says I have obsessive-compulsive tendencies. He misquotes me. He notes the "significant relief" I got from lidocaine injections even though I quit them because the lidocaine just numbed my head for four hours, and when it wore off, I got this squeezing headache that felt like my pain rebelling against the treatment. I devour every page, every footnote, weighing what each one says about me and whether these descriptions match the way I see myself. When Audrey opens the door, she says she's sorry for making me wait; she's been running late all day. "It's okay," I say. My voice lacks inflection. Usually, when I see Audrey, I'm upbeat—or, put in the terms Piven uses in his notes, I exhibit *high affect*. Today, I am weary, and I expend none of my usual effort to hide my dejection. I'm afraid that Audrey will think the central nervous system depressant she writes me depresses my psyche, too, so I try to appear fresh and bright at my appointments, gesticulating with energetic hands while I update her on my classes, joke about the oxy I watched skitter from between my fingers and into my printer, pretend that I prefer sitting at home to the reading or party my headaches most recently prevented me from attending. I tuck my hands between my thighs and let a dull expression settle on my face. I have not showered in three days. I am tired. I am depressed. This month, I don't find anything funny. My pain is not under control, and it's taking a toll on me. "I have to up my dose," I say. Audrey and I have been trying to keep me on four 5-milligram pills a day for the past six months, but I can't fully function on four 5-milligram pills a day. I tell her I'm exhausted by the running pill count I keep in my head and tired of suffering to make the numbers work. "And I can't write," I keep saying. "I'm in a writing program. I have to be able to write." Audrey asks me how much longer I have before I finish my MFA. I have a year and a half, but I'm adamant that it's not about school. "I need to write," I say. "I'm going crazy. I feel dead inside." I start to cry, and Audrey hands me a box of Kleenex. "This can't be my life. My head hurts all the time. And if I can't do the one thing I really care about…" I decide not to finish the sentence. I can't tell the person who writes me a potentially lethal drug that I think about death all the time. I wipe my eyes and shake it off. "I have to up my dose," I say again. Audrey writes me a prescription for 145 pills, fifteen more than I had the month before. But she has to refer me to pain management. If I need to up my dose, she explains, the practice needs to send me to an expert.

8. For as long as I can remember, I've been a writer. In kindergarten, I made my sisters and a friend perform my adaptation of *Little Women* in our living room (we never got around to staging *Anne of Green Gables*). After her dad died, the mom found a poem I'd written for him. She heaped praise on it, said it made her cry. I should have thanked her and let her keep the poem. Instead, I snapped at her for reading my stuff. On our family's first computer, I typed up something called "Sixth Grade is the Pits" and stuck a clipart piece of pizza on the title page. It's somewhere in the suitcases where I keep my novels. Mostly, I wrote novels. I spent hours cutting pictures out of magazines and filling index cards with characters' traits. My novels were almost invariably about girls a couple of years my senior who ran away from bad homes; the girls always met and fell for sweet, gentle older guys who offered up their couches to my reluctant protagonists. Sometimes I varied the formula: the girl met an asshole first, and his roommate or a coworker or a random man on the street took her under his wing when the first guy kicked her out or tried to fuck her. I don't know where these stories came from. Surely

they were escape fantasies, but why did I write so many versions? Why were the details so specific, and what do they say about me? I wrote those stories in middle school and early high school, when I also kept a giant bottle of Extra-Strength Tylenol in my locker. We were supposed to get permission from the school nurse to take any kind of medication, and I was always afraid someone would find my stash; I'd get in trouble, and it would go on my permanent record, a lie in which I wholly believed. I slipped pills into my pockets and walked to a water fountain like a bullet, the way I walk now when I just want everything to end. Pain made me different; it isolated me. I spent the school day in my head or in a book, and I spent my off time with friends to whom I never really explained the ways I hurt or alone in the bedroom I'd chosen specifically because its bathroom didn't connect to my sisters' rooms. I never called what I felt by its name, but I think I've always written from a place of depression, spurred on by pain I don't understand.

9. I walk into my house and beg someone to kill me. "Just let me die. I just want to die," I hiccup out between sobs. I don't know to whom I'm addressing my pleas. I don't believe in God or a sentient universe. No one and nothing will answer my call. I stand in my kitchen and scream. I don't use words. I scream twice, and then my head feels worse. I drop to my knees and ask again to die. "I don't want to do it anymore," I say. My voice is quiet and hoarse. I know I'm going to get off the floor. I know I'll wake up tomorrow. I can't inflict pain on myself, and I'm afraid of brain damage. If I tried to overdose and it didn't work, no one would write me a narcotic prescription again. These aren't suicidal thoughts. I'm not thinking about the best ways to kill myself. I don't really want to die. I just don't want to be alive. It's different.

10. When the new first-year MFAs arrived at the beginning of my second year, sometimes I'd look at them and see how young they really were: 22, 24,

25; even 27 felt young when set beside my 30. They possessed this tangible youth that I couldn't find in myself anymore; it felt like muscle, like a pumping vein, and also like vapor. I was jealous. Why didn't I do what I wanted when I still had that energy? I was incredulous. What did these people have to write about? Where was their self-doubt, their anxiety, their fucking cynicism? When I was 22, I thought academia could satisfy my need to document everything, to write it down and shape it. I did my MA in women's studies with the assumption that I'd go on to get a PhD and teach. But mostly I loved the research, constructing complex sentences and teasing out meaning in texts I examined and braided together. I wasn't really getting headaches anymore, or I didn't get them often. When I started taking David's Xanax and the opiates he tricked doctors into writing him and, after we broke up, smoking weed in my apartment every night, I stopped having all but occasional headaches. When I had them, I'd lay on my back in my hallway and cry. But, more often, I cried because I was lonely. Most of my friends had moved away, and I spent too much time by myself. But I couldn't be depressed, I told myself, because I was happy. I was in Gainesville. I loved Gainesville. There was always a party, and I could still drink without getting a migraine. I was focused and serious yet still young enough that I could snort a gram of cocaine on Thursday night and head straight for my computer on Friday morning to work on my thesis. I went to class stoned and still managed to speak coherently about Judith Butler. I published a paper. I presented papers at conferences. "And I could take days off to clean my apartment!" I told people while I applied to MFA programs. By then, I'd spent five years working for nonprofits, and I was exhausted. I remembered college and grad school as these oases of happiness. Those years feel like someone else's life. I thought that, when I went back to graduate school, I could be that person who did those things again. I thought I'd be able to drink with the new friends I'd make once I got off Suboxone and into an MFA program and didn't have headaches anymore. I thought I'd clean my house on my days off. But I couldn't drink, couldn't socialize, and my headaches didn't go away; I had to hire a maid service to make my apartment look presentable for my leasing company's quarterly inspection. I watched other people do grad school the way I'd done grad school, and I had no idea how their bodies withstood it. I couldn't remember ever being that young or any of the million ways I'd once been invincible.

11. The last time I didn't have a headache, I was on acid. The time before that, I'd eaten mushrooms. I chewed and swallowed a rubbery handful in the All-Saints dressing room and spent $612 on a leather jacket and a white sweater dress with a billowy skirt and structured top. I threw up in front of the Canal Street Q station, wiped my mouth, and rode the train for hours. I stared at the speckled subway floor that swirled beneath my boots. Something felt off. I kept checking my bag, convinced I'd lost something important. But I hadn't dropped a glove, misplaced my ID or a credit card, set down that $612 shopping bag and forgotten to pick it up. My pain had gone missing. My head felt flung open, like that first spring day when you can open your windows. I laughed in disbelief and awe, alone on a baby-blue bench. I touched my head, searching for the tender spots that weren't there anymore. I got off the train when I stopped recognizing street names, walked up to the sidewalk, lit a cigarette, and watched the smoke glitter in the light of a bodega's red neon sign. A guy in a black Navy pea coat told me I was in Queens. I'd have to ride all the way back up to 42nd Street to get a train back to Brooklyn. Unlike all the other times I'd fucked up my route or gotten off at the wrong stop, I didn't curse my stupidity or kick the thickly painted forest-green stanchions that lined the tracks. I went back down into the subway and waited unperturbed for the next uptown train. *So this is what it's like*, I thought, *to be a regular person.*

12. The day after I fill my new prescription, I get a migraine and my period. The migraine lasts four days, and for at least another week my headache is rigid and sickening; nothing touches it. I keep taking pills and hoping they'll make me feel better, but they don't. It's such a rookie mistake, wasting drugs on pain that's proved itself immune to them, and I'm angry at myself for having made it. I imagine my head as a bucket of vomit too heavy to turn over, like it's a separate entity that really could throw up if it wanted to. I'm cold in my bones even with tights on under my jeans. Even in my house with the heat on. Cold tenses my back and shoulder muscles, which strains my neck so my head absorbs the pressure. I have the pills I need now, but my head hurts too much, and I still can't write. I tell myself I'll feel better the next day and then the next day and the next until I do, sort of. I'm going to write if I have to take twice my dose. If I don't, my bones will break through my skin. I can feel them pushing and tearing, and I don't care anymore that there's no way my prescription will last more than 21 days. Audrey and I say my prescriptions should last 28. But I didn't get dependent on oxycodone again so that I could stay on the couch moaning. I got dependent on oxycodone again so I could live, so I could write. Audrey will have to understand.

13. I see Nancy a week later. I tell her maybe I feel better, but maybe I don't. I'm not sure. I cross my legs and lean forward with my elbows on my knees. "If I say this, you have to promise not to tell any of my doctors," I say. She nods. "I think it's the opiates. I think I feel like this because of the opiates." I would never say this to my mother. I've never really said it to myself. And it's more complicated than that, I explain to Nancy. "It's not like I wouldn't be depressed if I weren't taking them. I just think... Am I doing this to myself?" My voice breaks at the end of the question. "But what am I supposed to do?

I mean, do I think I'd feel better if I never got to not have a headache?" Nancy nods and says it's hard; the opiates likely do impact my moods. She holds her hands up like a scale. "But, you know, there's negatives to everything," she says. "You have to decide what's right for you. And you've got to get your pain under control if you're gonna deal with the other stuff." I shrug. I can't look at Nancy when she agrees with me. "I know," I say. I've been saying it for years.

14. I spent a year "clean" after I stopped taking opiates. I finished my Suboxone detox and moved from the mom's two-story house in Florida to my Depression-era two-bedroom in Virginia as though withdrawal were a simple reset button. The worst part was not the acute withdrawal. The acute withdrawal lasted ten days, maybe fourteen. Since I had someone to take care of me, acute withdrawal was like having a bad flu on vacation. I binge-watched the mom's premium cable and read all day. I ate only mint chocolate chip ice cream, lentil soup, and cheeseless pizzas topped with onions and black olives. I took the most sublime shits. I hurt all over the entire time, felt edgy and anxious despite not having to worry about the money the mom and I spent on my detox, missed work, oily hair, children or a spouse—not even a pet; the mom fed my cat when I couldn't get out of bed to do it myself. Acute withdrawal has a definitive beginning and fuzzy but palpable end. You know what you're getting into, how you should feel, what you're moving toward. Post-acute withdrawal creeps up on you even if you're expecting it. In post-acute withdrawal, you're feeling your brain reestablish connections you severed when you started giving it synthetic dopamine. You're listening to a voice in the back of your head whisper reminders that, eventually, you'll have to live like a person again. Post-acute withdrawal can last anywhere from a week or a month to years; for some people, it never ends. I was starting an MFA program in a month. I didn't have forever. I moved to Virginia exactly 30 days after I

slipped my last Suboxone tab under my tongue, and I still didn't feel like a person; I still had trouble living like one on my own. I spent my first semester and a half at Virginia Tech depressed and foggy and then despondent, sure I was one of the people who spend their entire lives in a post-acute withdrawal haze. Unless I was reading, I couldn't concentrate for more than 30 consecutive minutes. To sit at my computer and write strained my weakened muscles and still-recovering brain. I couldn't identify the words I needed to translate the images in my head onto a page. Some days, the images didn't even come. I had been admitted to a writing program and now I couldn't write. I didn't know this version of myself; I'd never not been able to do something. And I did do it, just slowly and with effort that took all the energy I had. None of my professors or peers knew I was still in withdrawal unless I mentioned it. But I recognized that something had gone missing in me even if the people around me didn't. They didn't know what had once been there, and neither did I, not fully. Whatever had absented itself—some aura or spark—I'd taken for granted when I had it. But I knew I didn't feel like anyone I'd ever been. When I started taking opiates again, I felt some piece of my self return to my body. That loss, whatever it was, still haunts me more than the easy misery of acute withdrawal. If I had to get off opiates again, I could handle the gradual taper and the week or two in bed, but the post-acute anxiety and emptiness, the disassociation from the traits I cram together and call *me* and from the craft that gives my life purpose and meaning—I know that lack too well to live in it again.

15. I used to look for myself in books and movies and academic literature. "Chronic daily headache" barely brings up results on Google. You have to wade through WebMD and Mayo Clinic pages on migraine before you find the pages actually dedicated to "Chronic Daily Headache," which are few

and usually generic, their information slim. I don't do it anymore. It's not worth it. Pain specialists tout their special cures—lidocaine injections and nerve blocks and reiki—but there isn't a cure for my pain. I can manage it. I can live with it. But I can't banish it. In New York, Paul always said, "There's not going to be a magic bullet." I tried to believe otherwise. I hoped for a brain tumor so that a surgeon could just cut the headaches out. I hoped for Topamax and amitriptyline. I hoped for the detox. I hoped for the lidocaine. I hoped until I couldn't hope anymore. There's only so much you can hope before your stores just dry up. My psychiatrist at Virginia Tech asked once if I was happy depending on pills to "get through the day." He has this tone of voice like he's condescending to you even when he's not; I yell at him all the time for the way his voice sounds, the implications it carries, even though I know now that he can't help it. This time it was the phrase "get through the day" that set me off. "You say that like I'm just taking this stuff to pass the time," I snapped. "I'm taking it for pain." I told him he couldn't talk to me that way until his head hurt all the time like mine did and he couldn't find anything else to do about it. Then I said I didn't mind at all taking oxycodone every day. "I'd be *happy* if everyone wasn't such a fucking fascist about it." I know that's not true, or not entirely, but I wish it were. I wish I could point at something and say, "Now that, *that* would make me happy." But I know that no such thing exists. I've accepted that I will always have headaches, that I can't sustain happiness, and I depend on that pessimism for survival. I've crawled to the edge of hope and found comfort in its absence. My pain, the loneliness it engenders, my sometimes hysterical despair, chronic melancholy, the anger like a still black lack in my chest—these things haven't and presumably won't go away. I've gotten used to things I never wanted to get used to, and from down here on the ground, hopelessness has proved the more prudent view.

CODEPENDENCE

1. "I can just tell you've got a million things in your head, and I know, like, nine of them," David says. He's closing the door to his room at Highland House, a bed and breakfast in Grayton Beach. I'm already on the porch, loading my one hitter with a pinch of the weed David brought me from Gainesville. I bend my knees into triangles on a white wood chaise that looks like a beach chair, but it's nice. Everything in David's hotel room is nice. The walls are mint green, the floors hardwood. The four-poster bed is so tall that even David has to catapult himself onto the mattress like a vaulting gymnast. A mirror on the east wall is framed in thick hammered metal, painted white and curved outward to form a shallow shelf. The shelf holds a mason jar filled with tiny, long-stemmed purple flowers and shells in a glass bowl. Dried starfish line the high windowsills. On the chest of drawers that stands against the western wall, David's computer sits beside his Suboxone bottle and a small TV. An angular sink juts from the wall in the bathroom, and above the toilet hangs a blond-wood shelf with a deceptive handle on its front. I'd tried to open it earlier and nearly pulled the thing off the wall. The handle doesn't connect to a drawer; it's just screwed on for show. David's needle, fitted with its safety-vest orange cap, reclines there beside miniature soaps and an intricately folded washcloth. Outside, there's another chaise like the one I'm in and a high table where David perches on a chair with long legs and a back so squat he looks like he might fall off it. Strings of fat white

bulbs hang loose and low from the roof, lit even at nearly three in the morning. Gulf waves shush us from a hidden shore. David has spent the last hour trying to make me come. He was so precise about it, almost clinical, pulling back my clitoral hood and pressing his fingertips to the exact right spots. Outside, David blames my inability to climax on oxycodone; I've been taking it again for a year now. "Maybe," I shrug. I pull on my pipe that looks like a cigarette. David pulls an actual cigarette from his red-and-white pack of Marlboros. "I was really close," I say. "I just… I don't know. I feel like I can't abandon myself anymore." David nods. I hold pot smoke in my lungs and let it out. Cough. "What are the nine things?" I ask. David takes my lighter and glances down at me over its flame. His brown eyes go wide and then narrow again. He looks like a zoo lion considering a curious child. "You said I have a million things in my head…," I prod. David steadies himself on the porch railing. "Oh, yeah," he says. He says he knows I'm trying to relax, and he says he knows I'm nervous because I haven't had sex in almost sixteen months. He says I'm chastising myself for taking so long and that I'm weirded out because this is really happening. He says he knows I'm trying to remember everything so I can write these scenes later. He says I'm scared I'm doing something that will hurt me. "How do you know all that?" I ask. "I know because I know you," David says. I don't look at him. I'm too nervous about the way I don't feel nervous even though I know I should, and I'm scared he'll use all the ways he knows me to pull me into the relationship I know he wants but that I'm not sure I do. All the uncertainty in my future renders me vulnerable to David's declarations of undying love and to the seductive ease with which we slip into our old roles after a dozen years apart. I take another drag from the one hitter and laugh my stoned laugh David likes to tease me about. "There it is," he says when he hears it: a laugh like the lazy waves we can hear but not see.

2. When I broke up with David in college, I told myself I wasn't allowed to date again until I made better decisions. Except I still don't make better decisions. I know because I've tried and failed. *How can I know what kinds of decisions I make if I don't make any?* I ask myself at irregular intervals before I venture off to decide the wrong thing. I never wanted what I could have, and I always decided to reach for it anyway. At 20, I wanted Tom, who made clear how unavailable he was by remaining exactly available enough to fuck my heart raw on and off for ten years. At 22, I wanted Ray, probably because he was unavailable; I could only see him when his band went on tour. We would never be a couple. I couldn't get my hopes up, and he couldn't let me down. We saw each other once or twice a year up until Ray quit touring in 2012. He settled in Portland, and I kept moving around. While I worked on my master's in women's studies and during the first two years I lived in New York, I wanted casual sex, and I wanted respect, but I couldn't get both at once. Now that I didn't want a relationship, the men I fucked assumed I did. No matter how little I wanted from him or how clearly I communicated that the desire was mine, the guy I slept with always woke up grinning like he'd pulled something over on me. I could walk up to a man in a bar and say, unprompted, "Wanna have sex?" and still, in the morning, he'd treat me like I'd fallen for his trick. I thought he'd fallen for mine.

3. I stumble out of the mom's Altima, clumsy and disoriented from a migraine and my grumbling stomach, so empty I press my hand against my abdomen and expect to touch my spine. David sits on a fence railing that looks a hundred years old. It's a short fence: enough of a barrier to suggest a separate space but not to actually create one. Behind it stands a white tent where Highland presumably holds beach weddings, but I can't see the beach from here. I'm wearing ankle-length gray pants with cuffed hems, a black camisole,

brown sandals, and my lucky wishbone necklace that looks gold but isn't. I've just driven over from the Zoo Gallery, where I still work when I'm in Florida. Before I left, I'd texted David to warn him about the migraine I could feel moving into my skull. The store reeks of incense and scented candles and old lady perfume. I've been there intermittently for thirteen years. I'm used to the smell. I don't think the store smells like anything until suddenly I do. The heavy incense dust and sick-sweet soy wax burn my nose and catch in my throat, and all of it mixes together in my sinuses and nauseates my head. When I can smell the Zoo, I know I'm ready to return to whatever city I'm calling home that year. But this year I'm not ready. I need more time to decide what I want with David, what I'm doing with him here. We haven't had sex, and I don't know that I want to. I'm afraid sex will wipe a dirty thumb over the picture of our relationship I keep framed inside my head. Sex might wash out the oversaturated joy our reunion has lent this summer. I know I'm getting the migraine because I can't rid the Zoo Gallery's smell from my pores or my clothes, because I've finished cleaning up after the customer who walked in three minutes before we would have closed and wrecked the place fretting over which linen tunics and wide-leg pants she should write a $2,200 check to pay for; I'm getting the migraine because I'm here at the hotel and have quit worrying about getting lost or about the lie I told the mom because she's hated David since 2002. The mom thinks David ruined my life, that I wouldn't take opiates for my headaches if I'd never taken them for fun with him. I want to tell her how scared I am that David might have been right when he said no one else would ever love me like he did, but I can't admit to myself how much I want her to talk me out of this, and I'm afraid she'll hate me, too, if I tell her where I really am and what I'm really doing. I'm late and starving, and now the stress releases as pain dripping into my brain like vinegar from a squeezed sponge. "I have to eat something," I say. "Like, a real meal." David lifts my purse off my shoulder. He takes a near-empty box of Wheat Thins from the crook of my arm and my water bottle out of my right hand. "We'll get you some food," he says. David sets my things inside the door and passes me the Ziploc bag he's filled with ice and wrapped in a hand towel. I press it to my skin until my skull is numb. "What do you want to eat?" David asks. He'd gone to the grocery store earlier that day and texted me the same question. *I can't ask you to feed me,* I texted back. *I'm too much trouble.* Now, David drives all over Grayton looking for food that won't trigger a new migraine or invite this one to settle in for the week. No meat. No cheese. No nuts or chocolate or dried things or fried things or smoked things or mangoes or shellfish. I'm making a tall order in a beach town at 10:30 p.m., but David promises he can fulfill it. While he's gone, I change into one of David's T-shirts and a pair of blue-plaid boxer shorts I take from his suitcase. I flatten my back under thick white blankets trimmed in lace and try to relax, ice over my eyes like a bandit's mask. David keeps calling to read menus to me so I can tell him why nothing on them works. He comes back with two spicy tuna rolls and edamame in Styrofoam boxes. "Shit, you were hungry," he says. I'm cramming sushi into my mouth and extracting soybeans with my teeth, precise as a surgical robot. I turn over onto my full stomach and let David rub my neck and shoulders and all down my back. "You're getting knotty again," he says. "Like, I'm never getting that one." He presses a spot between my shoulder blades. I make a sound like sex. When I'm sure the migraine won't settle, I let David turn me over and kiss me. I kiss him back, and we move like eels under the sheets. I feel guilty when I tell him I know I won't come tonight, but I'm bored, too; I'm over orgasms the way fashion bloggers are over high-low dresses. "You used to come so easy," he says, but I don't remember the way I climaxed at eighteen and nineteen. I remember how David hurt me in shitty motel rooms where he shot cocaine and hunched in corners, annoyed that I wanted to chatter chatter chatter because I'd snorted my share. I remember the money I spent on his doctors' visits and prescription pills, how my fingers sounded tapping on my steering wheel while I waited in dealers' driveways. I remember all the ways we could have died or been arrested and how it felt to have my heart stripped for parts one vessel at a time. "Did I?" I ask. I remember all the bad parts so well that it's hard to believe the nice things David tells me about those days or in all this care he couldn't offer me when he called himself my boyfriend.

4. When I tried to want the people I was supposed to want, I got bored or nagged or raped. In New York, I made an online dating profile and for the first time ever went on real dates. I tried hard to make the right choices. I gave chance after chance to a classics PhD student even though I always fell asleep before we got around to having sex; we'd make out, and I'd wake up on his shoulder at dawn, all my clothes still on. Being with Classics Guy reminded me of being with my friend Ben, a historian dissertating at Stony Brook whom I sometimes fucked. Ben was safe and kind and felt good inside me; we cared about each other, and we could talk all night, but we'd always lacked passion. On paper, both men made such appropriate partners, but in bed our movements felt workmanlike and bureaucratic, like math instead of chemistry. I fell hard for a recording engineer with blue eyes and a good beard and these adorable little long-haired dogs who sat on the couch and stared at me while I sucked their person's dick. When he was about to go down on me for the first time, he stopped and said, "Is your vagina clean?" We'd been hanging out for a little less than a month. My jeans were half off. My top was somewhere in my bedsheets. "Of course it's fucking clean," I said. "But it doesn't matter now." I sat up and groped around for my T-shirt, black with a big white feather printed on its front. "I don't know what's 'clean' to you. All I'll be able to

think about is whether you think I'm gross." I shouldn't have, but I cried. I got angry. I felt vulnerable, half-naked in bed with someone I'd liked a lot until he hurt my feelings. He said I was making too big a deal out of the question. I snorted. "Did I ever ask you if your dick was clean?" It was the last thing I know I said to him. I said yes to a home-cooked meal with Rick, who insisted on making dinner for me at his place on Long Island. I suggested we meet somewhere neutral and public the way women are supposed to in order to keep ourselves safe. But Rick persisted, and I gave in. He worked in finance. He owned his duplex and his car. The dad would have liked him. Which is to say that Rick was not my type, and I agreed to the date because my type had failed me. Still, I was nervous about going to a stranger's house all the way out on Long Island. I made Rick text my friend Leslie a picture of his driver's license. If anything bad happened, she would know where to find me and how to identify the man who'd chopped my body into pieces and thrown them in the Sound. I left Brooklyn before sunset. I wore a chunky black sweater, black leggings I used like long johns, black jeans, a black coat, chocolate-brown boots that zipped up to my knees. I rode the Q train to the LIRR at Atlantic Terminal, and I rode the LIRR to the station at which Rick had told me to disembark. He waited for me in a sleek black sports car, something obviously expensive, and he honked so I'd know where to go. The dinner was so unre-markable that I barely remember its constituent parts—rice, I think, and tiny diced vegetables and some kind of meat substitute or perhaps fish. "This is good," I said after I swallowed my first bland bite. While we ate, Rick told me about the stock-trading app he'd developed. He said it would make him a millionaire. He drew a chart on a napkin that was supposed to explain how the app worked, but he had to explain how the stock market worked, too. "I'm not going to get it," I said and took my plate to the kitchen. I rinsed it, set it in the sink, and walked over to my purse to get the weed I'd brought. Rick gave me his bowl to load while he flipped through his DVDs. He said he wanted to watch a movie. I bristled. I didn't want to watch a movie. "Watch a movie" meant that Rick wanted to fuck or at least make out a little, and I wasn't that interested. The trains back to Brooklyn quit running at five minutes to midnight, and it was already nearly 9:00 p.m. I told him I'd watch anything that wasn't scary, as if in abandoning my type and my instincts I had to abandon myself to this person entirely. Rick held up a DVD case I recognized: Johnny Depp on its front cover, title displayed in a gold gothic font. "Isn't that kind of scary?" I asked. "Kind of," Rick said. "But you're safe. I've got you." He flashed a smug entrepreneurial grin, gripped my shoulders with both his hands, and squeezed. I did not feel safe. I snuck an extra Klonopin and sat on the couch with my legs crossed. He kissed me maybe 20 minutes in. I put down the bowl we'd been passing and let him. I knew I didn't like him much; I thought I'd get in a little low-stakes pleasure, and then I could make him drive me to the train. But Rick wanted sex. I disguised my relief as disappointment when the condom in my purse didn't fit him, when he said he'd just ended a four-year relationship and wasn't used to keeping them around. I don't know why I even considered fucking him. I was lonely, I guess, and maybe I figured it didn't matter. Nothing mattered except my pills and my pain. My ears pricked at anything that might make me forget for any length of time that I hurt—things like another person's touch or an orgasm, even if proffered by someone I'd begun to actively dislike. But I wasn't going to fuck this random guy without a condom. "We can do other stuff," I said. I read dissatisfaction on Rick's face, but his hands tugged at my jeans anyway and pulled them down to my knees with the tights he expressed surprise at finding underneath. He fumbled around my dry labia, rubbing my skin in circles so vigorous I thought I might light on fire from the friction, and then he rammed his fingers into my vagina. I said it hurt. He slowed down, shifted position, and like a snap I was on the other side of his black leather sectional. He'd tried to stick his penis in me, as though I wouldn't notice the switch from digit to dick. Rick insisted I'd only felt his two fingers. "I'm not an idiot," I said. "I know what a penis feels like. That was not your fingers. That was your penis." I sniffled and pushed my hair out of my eyes and sat up and shook my leg like I do when I'm anxious. I put all my clothes back on, leggings included, and stepped out onto Rick's small balcony to smoke a cigarette. I considered exit strategies. I couldn't go home. It was 11:49. There was no way we'd make it to the train in six minutes. When I went back inside, Rick tried to start again where he'd left off. I pled exhaustion. Headache. I'd come straight from work, I lied, and I didn't usually stay up this late. But if I wanted to sleep, I had to do it there—or, I thought I did. I guess I could have asked Rick to drive me home, but I had myself convinced I was trapped, and I didn't know if he'd react badly or whether I should show him where I lived. I said I would sleep on the couch. "Don't be silly. Sleep in the bed," Rick said. I thought he meant to offer me his bedroom, that he would sleep on the couch. I removed only my jacket and cocooned myself inside his blankets: a clear sign, I thought, that nothing else would happen between us that night. I could hear Rick bumping around his guest bathroom. "I found a Magnum!" He called it out like a conquistador planting a flag. My stomach sunk into the mattress. I'd spent four hours dodging this man's advances—and so politely. He'd worn me down, ground me up like cow parts. I felt as if I were watching myself from a hole dug into the earth specifically for me. The night splits then. I remember faking sleep, but I don't remember saying anything when I pretended to startle awake. I don't remember taking off my clothes, and I don't remember Rick taking them off, either, but I remember getting dressed in the morning. I remember us horizontal on the bed, parallel to the pillows, his weight against my ribcage unbearable, but I don't remember how I got that way. I remember fixing my eyes on what I see in my head now as a wrought-iron cross hung on a lavender wall, but I don't remember if there actually was a lavender wall or a cross on a nail. I don't remember how much it hurt, but I remember I wasn't wet at all. I remember thinking I couldn't say anything or shove him off because I had two narcotic prescriptions in my purse, and I needed both. I thought if I resisted, this man who probably didn't think he was doing anything wrong would take my oxys and my Klonopin in retribution. I don't remember why that made sense—he didn't even know the pills were there— but it did at the time. I remember fearing the need to name what was happening. I did not say no, and I did not say yes. I didn't say anything. I barely moved. I cried and masked it with grunts that reflected real pain. I don't remember turning over to go to sleep, but I know I woke Rick in the morning and told him he had to drive me to the train. I stood by the stairs that led down to his front door and waited while he grumbled about the early hour. "I can't even have a minute to make coffee?" he said. I looked at the LIRR schedule I'd pulled up on my phone. If I didn't get this train, I'd be stuck there another hour. I lied about something I needed to do at home even though only my cats awaited me, and I'd left them with enough food to last a week. We exchanged no words on the ride to the station, but when we got there, Rick walked with me to the ticket kiosk. He slid his credit card into the machine. *How bad could it have been*, I thought, *if he's buying my train ticket?* I waited for the LIRR alone, toeing the bright yellow line that runs parallel to the tracks with my boot sole. I watched the floor rattle under me while the train chugged back to Brooklyn. I pulled thoughts from my head with deliberate effort as if the words had been submerged in balm. I tried to think in a rhythm that did not match the cutting pulse of my cunt. But each thought was the same thought: *my fault, my fault.* I'd let it happen, this sex I didn't want to have even as I had it. My therapist agreed. She said I'd made a bad decision, going to a strange man's house on Long Island. What did I expect?

5. "Reparations," I whisper into David's hair, which my college weed dealer cuts now. One of his hands strokes my labia and the other rests on my chest like he needs it for balance. I'm too tired, too stoned, to do anything but lie there. And I've been so lonely for so long. I don't want to think about what I should do and what I want to do and how what I do will make David feel. I want to receive affection, but I'm not ready to give my own, and I could never match the fearlessness with which David offers his: nothing concealed, so bare it's like his bones are showing. The pleasure paralyzes me. I used to think it felt so good when David touched me because he was the first to really do it. And yet more than 30 men have touched me the way David is touching me at 3:00 a.m. in this fancy beachfront hotel room, and I can't remember any of them making me feel like this. There is something special, a little bit magic, about David's fingers. When they're in me, my vagina feels huge, as if there's an ocean below my hip bones, and somewhere so deep down that humans haven't mapped it yet, an oyster worries sand into pearl. Maybe this is where the trouble starts. Maybe this is where it all started: I attributed that initial pulse to David alone and gave a man the power I wanted for myself. I have to say again that I can't come. "I'm too stoned or tired or something," I murmur. But I was right the first time: I left my ability to let go on Long Island. "I can't even come by myself anymore," I tell David when he falls beside me on the mattress. He frowns, wraps me in his arms. My eyes keep closing when I don't want them to, and I dig like a prairie dog into David's chest. For the first time ever, I wake up in the morning positioned exactly the way I fell asleep: pressed against David so hard I'm stiff when I stand.

6. It took me a long time to call what happened on Long Island *rape*. I didn't want to be a woman who regretted sex and called it rape. But I didn't regret it

the morning after. I regretted it as it happened, and I was too scared, if maybe impractically so, to say no. In my head, I called it *that time I had sex when I didn't want to*. I didn't talk about it for at least two months. I sent Leslie a text that said the date had gone *Eh, fine. Whatever*. I thanked her for acting as my safety net even though I hadn't used her; when she called, I didn't know what to say: "Nothing bad has happened yet, but I'm afraid it will"? Rick was standing right there. And then it got too late. The train schedule. The exhaustion. The fear. I told the story out loud for the first time at Tom's apartment. Tom moved to New York a few years before I did, and when I got there, he'd married a British heiress so she wouldn't be deported. He loved her, he said, but he'd never have gotten married again had Alana not gotten arrested when Occupy Wall Street shut down the Brooklyn Bridge. He called her the love of his life as if he had no idea how much it hurt me to hear those words uttered by the man I would then have called the love of mine. They kept their relationship open, but Alana wouldn't let Tom see me. I wasn't just some girl. I meant something to him. I was a threat. Until I ran into him at a summer barbecue a few months after I moved to the city, I hadn't spoken to Tom in almost two years. The last time we'd talked, I'd called him crying about the job I lost in D.C. "I can't deal with you right now," Tom said. He said it as though I were a bill he could put off paying, homework he didn't want to do. I threw my phone across my near-empty bedroom and deleted his number. In New York, we acted like it never happened. When Alana went out of town, Tom would invite me to hang out in their apartment for a day or two, doing coke and having sex and watching him get drunk. I told him about Rick because I needed to explain why I didn't want to fuck this time. "I had weird sex a while ago. I haven't felt right since," I said. I turned my face from his so he'd know I was crying but wouldn't have to see it. Tom hates it when I cry. But now he looked at me with worried eyes and asked me to tell him what had happened. I narrated the night I'd taken to calling The Long Island Incident. In my telling, I emphasized all the opportunities I'd had to stop it so that Tom wouldn't say what I knew he'd say. "Amy, that's rape. You were raped. You know that, right?" he asked. I told him he was wrong. "I had sex when I didn't want to. It's not the same thing." Tom laughed the way one might laugh at something sad and at the same time ridiculous, like a kitten stuck on top of a refrigerator. "Listen to what you just said. 'Had sex when I didn't want to' is sort of the definition of rape." I wanted him to take it back. If Tom called it rape, I had to deal with it as *rape* and not *sex I didn't want to have*. The word matters. But when I use the word, I feel like I'm stealing it from women who did say no, women violated in ways more serious than the way Rick violated me. If my experience is rape, what is rape that involves real violence: women beaten, penetrated by broken beer bottles or knives? Tom said it didn't matter. I hadn't given consent. Rape was rape. Did I want a bunch of anarchists to go fuck the guy up? I thought about it. I hadn't deleted the picture of his driver's license from my phone. I had his address, his full name. "I'd rather not," I said. Rick probably didn't even know what he'd done. He was an asshole, not a monster. But he didn't need to be a monster to treat my obvious discomfort, my objections, the clothes I kept putting back on like they were obstacles to overcome. Sometimes I wish I'd said, "Yeah, do it." Sometimes I wish I'd let the weight fall on him more heavily than it fell on me.

7. In the morning, David brings me coffee and lets me have the last of the cinnamon muffins he bought at Publix the day before. We smoke cigarettes on the porch. It's early, and no one else is out. I sit in David's lap on the chaise. The air still holds the night's breeze. "I want to have sex when we go inside," I whisper into David's ear. I can't locate the thing that's changed. Maybe it's just David. Or it's the old stories we've been telling, how his

face shifts from pensive to sheepish to cat-like when I tease him for the way he misremembers our past. Maybe it's the ice pack he made and that my head feels better now, opioid-soothed and warm from the morning sun. Maybe I just want to feel a man's weight on me, to remember what it's like to fuck someone who loves me. We're fucking sitting up, facing each other, his legs crossed and mine straddling his lap, when someone from housekeeping walks in. Doesn't even knock on the door. I don't look. David does. ("That lady nodded at me," he'll say later, "like, 'Good job, kid.'") We laugh, keep going. David asks if I want to switch places, him on top and me beneath him. "You know how I like an excuse to be lazy," I say. Usually missionary hurts, but it doesn't now; it only hurts when David bends my legs into a position they can't maintain. I have to tell him to stop.

8. The first time I tried to have sex after The Long Island Incident, I had a panic attack more intense than any since my first. It was my second date with a musician and studio technician who was funny and easy going, sweet and a little soft around the middle. He got up to fetch a condom, and as soon as he disappeared behind the other side of the door, my left arm started throbbing the way it does when a panic attack warns me it's coming. By the time the guy got back, I'd downed three Klonopin and was sitting on the floor beside his bed breathing hard and rubbing my hand in circles over my ribcage, where it felt like my heart was bruising the inside of my chest. "Are you okay?" he asked. I kept my eyes on the floor. "Panic attack," I said. I shook him off when he tried to touch me and climbed the stairs up to the roof. When I got back inside, I asked my date to call a car; I was in Bushwick and didn't have numbers for the taxi services there. "Just lay here a minute and see if you feel better," he said. "I don't want to put you in a cab like this." I said that was my decision, and I'd decided I wanted to go home. "Hang on. I'll call in a second.

Just let me hold you for a little bit." In retrospect those words sound creepy, like the words with which a grownup lures a reluctant child into his lap, and it was a stupid thing to say, to think, an oblivious offer—as if this relative stranger's arms meant a single thing to me or differed at all from the ones that had given me cause to panic in the first place. But I crawled onto his mattress anyway and started counting off the ten minutes I'd determined should pass before I would say again that I wanted a car. I passed out in less than five. In the morning, I woke up furious. How could I have let someone do this to me again? How could I have done it to myself? I pretended I wasn't angry as I climbed into the black SUV he called for me after we'd drunk our coffee. The guy didn't call me again, and I didn't call him. Even though I think he was trying to be nice, his refusal to listen to what I was saying reminded me too much of the last time I'd let someone hurt me because I'd felt isolated and vulnerable and too insecure to insist.

9. *Kari… I made out with David,* I texted Kari after the first time I saw David that summer. He'd come back to Niceville, he said, because he needed a break from Gainesville. Kari lives in Minneapolis. She'd finished our MFA program that spring, a year before me, and would start a PhD at the University of Minnesota in the fall. She knows about David because she read my writing about him in the workshops we took together. I hadn't planned to tell anyone I'd made out with David, but I told Kari because she reads my life as carefully as she reads my writing, and when the two collide, she wants to know all about it. She would want, I thought, to know that I'd gone over to David's grandmother's house and kissed him in the basement bedroom where he and I used to mess around thirteen years earlier. She would know exactly the kind of mistake I was making and whether I should keep making it. Kari texted back a day later. *Ahh how did this happen?? How do you feel about it now?* I struggled

to answer her questions. I answer them every time I see David or don't, every time I tell the mom I'm going to a party no one's throwing or hanging out with a friend who doesn't know she's hanging out with me. Had I answered Kari's questions directly, honestly, I'd have had to tell her that I didn't really know how I felt about David, but I'd missed affection and intimacy too much to resist a familiar mistake.

10. My cell number hasn't changed since I was seventeen. You can still reach me at the same number David wrote on a slip of paper the day we met; it's programmed into his brain cells, typed into some synapse that the proper proportion of adrenaline and need conspire to activate. In August 2011, during my second year in New York, I stood in a crowd on the Union Pool porch, waiting for some friends to play a show. I noticed I'd missed a phone call from a number with an 850 area code. Eight-five-zero means Okaloosa County, means home. I bent over, finger to one ear, and tried to make out the voicemail. "An inmate in the Okaloosa County Department of Corrections is attempting to contact you," said a woman's robotic voice. I didn't have to guess which inmate. The last time I'd seen David had been in a picture my not-yet-former brother-in-law took with his cell phone and sent to mine: David stands in a grassy median between the Silver Sands Outlet Mall, where we once got caught making out on a security guard's golf cart, and a Shell gas station on the eastern edge of Walton County holding a sign above his head that reads *GOING OUT OF BUSINESS SALE!! 50% OFF MATTRESSES!!* By the time David called me from jail, we hadn't talked in at least two years. Until about 2009, I could claim the restraining order I took out on him in 2006 still prohibited contact, and he'd back off, unsure as to whether I'd renewed it or was capable now of lying to him in the same ways he'd lied to me. I kept calling the jail, trying to confirm my suspicion, but no one would tell me which inmate

had attempted to contact me. David called the next night around the same time. We didn't talk about why he was there. I'd Google his name later and learn that he was there on principal to theft charges. "Principal to theft" means that David dispatched someone else to burgle the house of a drug dealer who owed him money, and the someone else snitched when he got caught trying to sell electronics—laptops, a TV, some gaming consoles—that the drug dealer had reported stolen. David's mom was exasperated. She wouldn't call a bondsman. She would make him detox in a cell while he waited for his court date. I wrote David long letters filled with details about my days at work, my headaches and doctors' appointments, and my nights alone or out in the city; I asked questions about his cellmates and routines and plans for the future. He wrote me notes composed in hurried pencil marks on the notebook paper I sent with my correspondence; David didn't have commissary money to buy his own. His writing was almost illegible. The sentences never quite made sense. He didn't answer my questions or react to my stories. He was coming off opiates and Xanax. He was reading Kafka and Upton Sinclair and John Grisham and *The Hunger Games*—anything the prison library had. He was making plans for when he transferred to and then out of a halfway house, but the plans changed with each letter he sent. After he'd spent a couple of years in prison, the court ordered David to the Phoenix House in Citra, just south of Gainesville. I visited him there once. I was on Suboxone, living with the mom, waiting to hear back about MFA applications. I'd gone to Gainesville to see friends, and on my way back to Destin, I drove 45 minutes out of my way to spend David's visitation hour with him. We walked through the facility, which looked like an abandoned elementary school attached to dilapidating dorms, and sat in the grass outside catching up. His prison stories were all new to me since he hadn't put them in his letters. David looked new to me, too, in a plaid button-up shirt, navy-blue slacks, and wire-rimmed glasses. His eyes were clear and his pupils bigger than mine. Someone had cut his hair a little too short, but he looked good off opiates. He was still funny, still charming. You could still hear David's drug history in his speech, but his voice was soft and his words were kind. He thanked me for coming and for my letters, told me funny anecdotes about the other guys at Phoenix House, asked me how I was and actually listened when I told him. We started talking on the phone when his phone had minutes on it. After he'd finished his stint in the halfway house, he moved to Gainesville. He got a regular phone plan, and we talked more often and more intimately. I listened to him tell me he wasn't going to do drugs anymore and then listened to him tell me about the drugs he'd done the night before. I doled out dating advice. David had started seeing a bartender at Common Grounds, my favorite bar when I was in college, and they were making plans to live together before he'd even finished his Phoenix House tenure. "Don't move in with her," I told him. "You need some David time. You need time to figure out what you're like when you're not in jail or somebody's boyfriend." Since I'd known him, David had always been in jail or somebody's boyfriend or both. A month or three later, when he broke up with the bartender, I said I'd told him so. He said he'd recommit to David Time, and then he started dating someone new. "You don't know how to be alone. You *always* have a girlfriend," I snapped when he tried to relate to my loneliness. "I haven't had sex in two weeks," he said, and I laughed, said, "Get back to me after a year and a half." David commiserated with me when pain doctors refused to write my pills because I refused to let them inject lidocaine and cortisol into my occipital nerve. David said, "See, you did it," when Audrey declared pain-management doctors impossible and convinced the family doctor she works for to write the prescriptions himself. David played the part of my boyfriend well enough that I agreed to see him when we were both in the Panhandle during my second MFA summer. I'd be in Destin, working at the

Zoo Gallery and living with the mom, until I ran out of my 90-day oxy supply in late July. David would visit Niceville in June. He figured he'd stay a month. Did I want to hang out? I did, I said. And could he bring me some pills? I was low on mine. I'd overtaken them so I could finish the first draft of my thesis. David said he'd get me four instant-release oxycodone pills, 80 mg each, from a woman he knew who had full-blown AIDS. She would die in September. We should have known. Not since the early 2000s have doctors in South Florida written 80 mg instant-release oxycodone pills to people who aren't dying. Eighties are so rare I thought they'd been discontinued. David gave me the pills in his grandmother's basement. We sat in near darkness, nestled beneath the brick house his late grandfather built on the Niceville side of the Choctawhatchee Bay after World War II. I got out my pill splitter and halved one of the round, green oxys. David shot his. I meant to save my other half, but I took it within a couple of hours; taking twice my daily dose was the only way I could get even a little bit high, and I couldn't watch David get high without getting high, too. We lay on a futon in the den beside his younger brother's bedroom and made out like teenagers. I knew I would do it before I got there. I didn't want David back. I just wanted to displace the growling loneliness that slept beneath my ribs and rattled awake at David's voice on the phone. I kept looking at David and laughing. "What?" he'd ask. "I don't know," I lied. Being with him like that felt surreal, impossible, like I'd tripped backward into a time when I didn't have headaches and still took drugs for fun. "I never thought I'd kiss you again," David kept saying. "Me neither," I said. I wrestled with whether I wanted to have sex with him even though neither of us had suggested it. David hadn't even joked about it. But I let myself get close to David again because I had no idea how I really felt about it, and I wanted to find out.

11. A lot of bad things happened in New York because I was alone. Or, I let

myself establish habits I wouldn't have elsewhere. All my friends were couples. I resented their neat living rooms and neat lives, their cute couple stories and the way they fit together like Tetris pieces. Beside theirs, my life looked as inadequate as my single-person hodgepodge plates placed beside a full kitchenware set. Still, every other weekend or so, I rode the Q to Union Station, switched to the L, got off at the Bedford stop, and took a left turn and two rights to sit down for big dinners Harry cooked in the Williamsburg apartment he shared with Jen, his partner and my best friend from college. The other guests were other couples: some combination of Emily and Ahmed, Leslie and Eric, Jen's brother Michael and his girlfriend Ann, and our married friends Jay and Jackie. I listened to them raise their voices over the fan above the stove and the crack and sizzle of heated olive oil. They held glasses of wine I couldn't drink and nibbled at Trader Joe's cheese plates I couldn't eat. Harry said to me one night that Jen waited in line at Trader Joe's while he did their shopping. He was stirring a marinara sauce into which he'd dumped a pound of clams he'd bought there. "That's smart," I said. I hadn't bought anything at a Trader Joe's since I'd lost my job and left California two years earlier. Trader Joe's had the best selection of migraine-safe foods and meat replacements, but the lines in the New York stores often snaked out the doors. I declined to mention that, because I had no extra person to help with the bags, the amount of food I could carry alone didn't justify veering an hour off my route from work to home. Or that, actually, I hadn't been able to grocery shop anywhere without triggering a panic attack since the afternoon in 2009 when I'd driven down the road that wound up to my garage apartment in the mountains outside Santa Cruz to shop at the Scotts Valley Market. The woman who bagged my items looked at me with a pity I might have imagined, but I felt ashamed in a way I can't explain except to say that it seemed as if she knew I spent all my time alone in pajamas. Almost every time we talked on the phone when I lived in New York, the mom said something about the Western Beef I could practically see from my Crown Heights studio. She'd found it when she helped me move to Brooklyn in March of 2010. "That's the nicest grocery store," she said again and again. And for months I went there every Saturday. I bought beets and fennel and big white-bread buns and kale and spaghetti sauce and pasta and couscous, my heart flicking on and off like the store's bad fluorescent lighting. I cooked myself single-pot meals and brought them to work in Tupperware containers that I washed in preparation for each upcoming day. I made involved sandwiches on weekend afternoons, toasting bread and sautéing eggplant slices, salting my tomatoes, tearing sprigs off bunches of rosemary. And then I couldn't anymore. I don't remember what changed or exactly when it did, but by 2011, I'd quit bringing my lunch to work and started buying $9 veggie subs from a Lenny's near my office or $1.99 microwavable soups from the Duane Reade across the street. I never told Harry that his pasta dishes or seafood casseroles were the first real meals I'd eaten in a week. I almost always left his and Jen's apartment when everyone else had finished their food and started on their third drinks. I wound through the hipster-crowded streets and descended the stairs at the Bedford L station, bound for home at the same time other people my age were climbing aboveground to begin their Saturday nights. I pretended I didn't envy their late starts and too-loud laughter just as I hid the jealous way I envied my friends' apparent happiness, good health, and stable partners. Coupledom seemed to imbue their lives with a corresponding ease and weight that mine lacked. I was too embarrassed to admit I felt left out, almost freakish, because I didn't have a person with whom to navigate a world that, apparently, only I experienced as dystopian. But my seething loneliness injected into weekend brunches and nights out a jagged dread and this hollow-boned insecurity that exhausted me. I no longer fit with the people who knew me best. I couldn't talk about the way I hurt. When I did, the people listening treated my chronic headaches as though they were stubbed toes, the pain's unrelenting intensity secondary to the pills I used to relieve it. Everyone I knew became an expert on pain. I needed exercise, vitamins, yoga, meditation: anything but the oxys I took so I could sit up and listen to people spout off cures they'd read about on the internet. To avoid talking about or exacerbating my headaches, I shuttered myself inside my apartment. I blamed the heat in the summer, and in the winter, I said it was too cold to go out. But, really, I was too depressed, too angry, too miserable to pry my body off my bed and make light conversation. I cried when I woke up and while I got dressed for work. I hid in my office building's bathroom stalls and cried after lunch, anticipating what my boss would find defective in me next. I cried in front of my doctor and every therapist I ever saw, even the ones I only tried out once for free. When I got home, my cat Patch would jump on the bed and wait for me to change into sweatpants so we could lie horizontal together and watch TV. I cried at her devotion and my predictability. The morning she died, I took her body to the Humane Society alone on the subway, eyes red behind wide black glasses. "Dead cat," I said when people tried to steal Patch's seat. I took up subway seats like the city owed me. I let my apartment get so messy I couldn't let anyone into it. Roaches took up residence in my microwave, and I didn't set out traps until I found one crawling on my pillow like a hotel chocolate. I thought about how I might die and make it look like an accident. When I told my therapist I was tired of being alone and sick of dating, that my life had become an unmanageable secret, she said I should ask my friends for help when I needed it. I only asked once. I'd woken up puking with a migraine and couldn't get on the train to pick up my clonidine. The pills were at the Beth Israel Duane Reade, right outside the Union Square L stop. Jen could have been at the pharmacy in fifteen minutes. Instead, she asked me if Duane Reade delivered; if it didn't, she suggested I call an errand service. But Duane Reade didn't deliver, and the errand services needed 24-hour notice. I said I'd look further into it, put my phone on vibrate, set an ice pack on my head, and took a nap. I woke up to a tight, furious fist knocking on my door. When I opened it, I found a stubby police officer standing at the threshold. He wanted to come in. "I'm fine. I just have a headache," I said. "Well, you might want to call your friends," he said. "They think you're dead." When I didn't answer my phone, I found out later, Jen had called Emily in a panic, and Emily and Ahmed told her to dispatch the cops to my house. I dressed and picked up the clonidine myself, the migraine still battering my skull and vomit still caught in my throat.

12. "I think I could take good care of you," David says. "I know it sounds weird, but I liked—I mean, I didn't *like* seeing you in pain, but I liked making you that ice pack. I liked being there when you needed somebody." David and I are sitting in his grandmother's minivan, parked in the back of the Grand Boulevard Shopping Center's parking lot. I've just gotten off work. We have fifteen or twenty minutes to talk and smoke cigarettes, and then I'll need to drive home to the mom's house. I'm smoking weed out of my one hitter, and David's smoking a Marlboro Red. I don't know how to reply to his pronouncement. I've been worried lately that I am too much. My loneliness is too much, and I've adapted to it too well; too many years on my own have turned me too particular, too singular, too attuned to trouble and too ready, too willing, even grateful, to escape it rather than sit still and ride out the initial turmoil endemic to new relationships. And yet I cannot get enough affection, the hole dug by too many romantic missteps and solitary nights too deep for one man to fill. When I talk in my therapy group at Virginia Tech's Cook Counseling Center, people tell me I take up too much space, and they're right: my need is too big for any space to hold. My depression is too much, and my

anxiety is too much; the ways my moods and emotions, my distress and desire, shift and swing and sink into me like teeth make me too unstable a person with whom to settle down. Most of all, my headaches are too much. It's too much to ask that someone love me and my headaches, too. But David loves my headaches. He's so careful with them, tender like he's stroking the inside of my skull. "I was scared," he says, flicking the ash on the end of his cigarette out the van's cracked-open window. "Scared of what?" I ask. "Headaches are a big part of your life. I didn't know how I would handle it," he says. "You did well," I tell him. But the worry—I'm too much; my headaches are too much— nags at me as I tap my one hitter against my palm to clean out its bowl. I'm relieved to hear that at least someone is willing to deal with my pain, but it also stings when David says he feared he couldn't. Because if David, who already loves me, worried about whether he could love me and my headaches, too, I know I'm right to worry about how other men will react when I admit that I have a headache all the time, that sometimes the headache is a migraine, and that it is always awful.

13. David and I make a plan. We'll keep talking the way we've been talking, but now we can talk about sex, too. He will visit Blacksburg in August. I'll finish my MFA in nine months and move to a new city, and David will move to the place I pick. We will not live together, at least not right away. David will date me the way he'd date me if he hadn't dated me when I was eighteen, when he didn't know how to love me without hurting me on purpose. In our new city, we will set the ways in which he is different now against the ways in which I am different now. We'll assess how well each person's new pieces fit the other's and make a new plan from there. I know while we devise this plan that we are essentially arranging a wedding. We even talk about marriage once. "I don't need the piece of paper," David says, and I say, "I might. You

know, if we get divorced." We aren't even half joking. That David and I will move somewhere and see what we are like there feels inevitable and right and totally fucked. Sometimes I think David so thoroughly fractured my romantic foundations that he owes me the kind of healthy, stable relationship I still feel too broken to build with someone else. Other times, I think I've agreed to a plan that's worse for me than all my bad decisions combined; this plan, I think, will drag me down. I could spend the rest of my life wondering whether someone else might have loved me as much as David says he does. David knows I'm less sure about our future than he is. I tell him I worry about what will happen when I tell my parents. I worry that, if he gets off the low dose of Suboxone he takes now so he won't start shooting heroin again, he'll steal my oxys when—not if—he relapses. Telling David these things scares me. I'm afraid he'll say he doesn't want to deal with my doubts, that it isn't fair that I'm not sure about him when he is so sure about me. The plan David and I devise will complete a set of blueprints we started drawing over a decade ago and that I'm no longer sure I want to finish. I've drawn these plans before. I know what happens when all the corners meet and the circles close: I lose.

14. David drives up to Blacksburg in August to visit for four nights and five days. I'm nervous. We haven't spent this much time alone together since I was in college, and I am different now. I'm harder to be around. I know my headaches and I demand too much patience, too much empathy, too much flexibility and too much rigidity, too much care, too much quiet—too much to name. The names are: *I'm sorry, but I have to break our plans tonight. The bar is too loud, too bright; let's stay in and smoke a bowl instead, but—oh, yeah—my house looks like seven of me are squatting in the living room, so please don't say anything about the cat hair and the greasy paper plates, the cigarette butts and unopened mail. Do we have to keep the lamp on? Yes, I'm teaching in sunglasses today. No, there's*

nothing I can eat on this menu. I can't leave the house when my head feels like this. If you're going in the kitchen, could you get my ice pack from the fridge? I'm turning down the brightness on the TV. Are you sure we need that light? But when I name the things I need from David, he jumps up to fill a Ziploc bag with ice. He wraps it in a washcloth and refills the plastic ice trays. He stacks them like Jenga blocks in the freezer. He asks what else he can do. He unplugs a lamp and fumbles toward my futon, where I'm washed in the TV's glow. I adjust the ice pack on my head. David gropes in the dark for his cigarettes. I know where mine are. I live in the dark. I know where on the floor sits every pile of papers, every book or errant boot, every cereal box and carton of American Spirits and grocery bag I've stuffed full of trash; I never trip even when all the rooms are pitch black. I know how to pick out the bottle that contains the pill I need without looking at the label. I know it's weird to ask someone else to exist like this, even someone who is visiting my home, and usually I don't; I turn on lights and try to make my living room look inhabited by an able-headed person. It is nice to not need to lie like that. It is nice to burrow into David's lap, ice pack sliding down my neck, and watch the episode of *Grey's Anatomy* I missed while we were out with my MFA friends on Thursday night. He was so charming, and each of my friends is so irresponsible and romantic that I think they all fell a little bit in love with him, too. To stay at the bar until midnight, I had to take one of the 15 mg oxys that David brought me and snort some of his Adderall. I know he's taken more than his allotted dose this month, and it is nice of him to offer me his drugs. I let him turn on lights so he can see to shoot up his Suboxone even though I hate that he shoots up his Suboxone, and the light makes me feel more alone than the needle I won't use. Late at night, while I sleep and he can't, David does my dishes and tidies up my apartment. He fixes my screen door. I say, "Thank you so much" and "You didn't have to clean the house," but David claims it's nothing, he likes doing it, he wants to.

I think about the way I live—in darkness, in solitude, in mess, in pain—and that perhaps I don't have a choice, that I have to be with this one person, David, the only man who wants to take care of me and maybe can. But David and I bicker the way we did through those black phones in the Alachua County Jail. I don't like the way he walks outside to smoke at the end of an argument without saying anything to me. I don't like hearing him wince and inhale through his teeth when he misses a vein. I don't like how he's always all over my apartment, and I don't like how he leaves in the morning to walk around my neighborhood by himself. His visit is supposed to serve as a sort of trial run, and now I feel around David the way I've felt around the couple of men I've dated since that night on Long Island: trapped, indebted, furious, feral, ungracious, ungrateful, guilty, unmoored.

15. I've just called Kari, Jen, Sara, Lindsey, Nora, both Emilys. Not one of my friends is answering her phone. I'm frantic, convinced I've already cosigned the lease on the codependent life I'll lead with David if I stick to our plan. I'm sure I've missed my chance to tell David that I'm not scared or uncertain but positive that dating him again is a mistake so huge it will devour me. It's a mistake because it will devour me. David will devour me, and I won't know until I'm drowning in his entrails. We'll get so tangled up that I'll only know the blood and guts are his when I've bled so much that I'm out of blood and guts to give. The mistake is that I'll give David everything; nothing will belong only to me. I know I'll make the mistake if I don't back out right now. Exactly now. It's late September. David's supposed to visit Blacksburg again in less than two weeks. If he does, I'll spend all week faking it, and David will know. I'll hurt us both trying to make him believe in something I don't anymore. *Have you booked your ticket?* I ask in a text message. *I'm not rushing you. I think I need to think about it. I just got really upset, and I don't want to get into it now*

and make you upset, but I don't want to make you spend that money if I'm thinking what I think I'm thinking. I hit send. My text is not cryptic. David has to know what it means. Before he responds, Kari returns my call. I read her a paragraph from this essay: the second half of #13. Writing this essay, I tell her, changed my mind. I started it hopeful, so sure of its end, and now I'm in a panic spiral with no idea as to its final shape. I keep seeing the mom in a pearl-white suit. She's sitting in the front pew at my courthouse wedding. She smiles as I stand beside my hypothetical groom, whom she loves because she sees how happy he makes me. When the groom morphs into David, the mom frowns, stands up, turns around, walks away. I try to run after her, but I can't move; David has his hand around my arm. That image is why I called Kari first: she and her mum, as she calls her mother, are closer than any parent and child I know. "Your mom loves you more than you can fathom," David said once when I told him I wanted the mom to like my boyfriend. "She'll accept it." He didn't get why I want more than the mom's grudging acceptance. More than the mom being disappointed in me for choosing David, I'm afraid she'll be disappointed for me. She'll know what I'm missing because she had exciting boyfriends before she married the dad: guys who flew planes, congressional aides, hot rednecks. David thinks the mom is boring, conventional, that she wants me to marry a banker or something. He thinks that, when I say I want the mom to like my boyfriend, I'm saying I'm willing to sacrifice my own happiness to make someone else happy. But Kari knows exactly what I mean. When I finish reading, she says, "Okay. I don't want to make your problem about me, but there's so much in there that sounds just like me and Nick." I hear Kari speak in her problem-solving voice, and weights lift from every nerve ending in my nerved-up body. I can barely hear beneath the din of my relief. "We'd just been together for so long, I felt like I was supposed to stay with him," she's saying of her ex-boyfriend. "And he always had some drama or problem

I felt like I had to solve. I was always really stressed out, and I couldn't talk to my mum about it because I didn't want to make her think less of him than she already did." Kari describes the way she felt when she started dating a new guy in Minneapolis. "I was like, 'Oh, people can be together because they *want* to be together, not because they *need* to.'" I keep saying, "Yeah" and "Oh my god" and "Totally." I keep saying, "Thank you." Over and over. "Thank you."

16. In his grandmother's van, David told me that his memories and emotions solidify into egg-shaped objects that form in his stomach and sink into his intestines. The eggs glow. He can take them out when he wants to and feel what he felt when each egg formed. "No matter what happens," he told me, "I'll always be glad I got to spend this time with you." Even if I decided I hated him the next day, he'd say, he would still love me. He would always love me. He wouldn't be mad if I changed my mind. "You'll have your egg," I'd joke when I still believed in the plan. But I didn't anymore, and despite all his reassurances, I was scared to tell David. He called me almost exactly when I hung up with Kari and asked about the text I'd sent, what I'd meant. "I don't want you to visit," I said. "I don't want to do this anymore." I said these words without emotion, slowly, like a soap-opera protagonist coming out of a coma. I'd hoped to sound sad, but I wasn't; I was certain. I resented David for letting me fall back on him, and I was angry at myself for doing it. David thought I was just nervous about his visit. "It's not the visit," I kept saying. "It's every-thing. It's you." I don't remember what David said. I was too focused on my lines, on communicating my fears in a way that didn't sound cruel or irreso-lute, to concentrate on how their recipient reacted. What he said didn't matter. Nothing he could have said would have changed my mind. I wanted David to hear that, to understand that I loved him but knew I could never relax into a relationship with someone for whom I'd have to sacrifice so much of what

I wanted. He was disappointed but not angry, and he didn't seem surprised. Of everything David said, I'm only sure I heard him tell me that he'd felt my apprehension. Before we hung up, we both said, "I love you," and I said, "I think I need us to not talk for a while." I ended the call and got up from my desk chair exhausted, my whole body creaking under the weight.

17. I never threw out the little shooting gallery David set up on the desk in my living room when he visited in August. I dismantle it in the middle of October, about three weeks after our phone call. We still aren't talking. I pick up the pill bottle David kept filled with clean water and the pill bottle into which he'd squirted dirty water and blood. I pick up the bottle cap where he dissolved his Suboxone in water, Q-tip cottons, the hollow stem of a red pen, my only non-disposable spoon. David had taken with him his syringe and the needle he'd used, so dull he had trouble hitting even his good veins. I bend to retrieve its orange cap, the color muted by dust and my cat's gray-and-white hair. I don't linger over any of the items. I toss the bottles into a grocery bag full of Coke cans and the cap and cottons into an empty kitty-litter carton. The spoon goes in the sink. I didn't keep the bottles and the cottons and the spoon in their places to keep a part of David present with me in my apartment; I just couldn't muster the energy to figure out what was what and how to discard it properly. But now all the bottles are emptied of water and covered in a thin white crust, and I don't have any decisions left to make.

ACKNOWLEDGMENTS

I want to thank Brian Blanchfield for choosing this manuscript; I entered the Cleveland State University Center's 2018 Essay Collection Competition because I love his writing, and I am grateful that he saw something special in mine. My editors, Caryl Pagel and Hilary Plum, really understood the book and its aims, and I know it ended up in the right hands; I appreciate their insightful, intelligent, and caring editorial guidance. I especially want to thank Caryl for our phone calls. And major thanks to Silas Breaux for making the map and symbols in "Pharmacies of New York."

This book would not exist without Matthew Vollmer. I conceived of its form and arc in his creative nonfiction workshop at Virginia Tech, and the medicine cabinet I made as my final project remains the only outline from which I've been able to work (thanks, Scott Fralin and Brian Craig, for helping me make all the stuff). Matthew's empathy, humor, and confidence in my vision; his patience with my freakouts and long emails; his excitement about the project; and his friendship mean more to me than I can express. I also want to thank Ed Falco and Katrina Powell for their notes and encouragement; Fred D'Aguiar for his enthusiasm; Erika Meitner, Jeff Mann, and Lucinda Roy for giving me space to work out these themes and pieces in their workshops; and all my MFA peers, especially Emily Dhatt (and her partner Robby White), Freddy Fuentes, Amy Marengo, Keri Campeau, Soraya Palmer, Xandria Phillips, Nora Salem, Sara Sheiner, Lisa Summe, my little brother Joe Truscello, and Sam Woodworth; Sally Wieringa and Bridget Szerszynski also deserve thanks for keeping the program running. Trysh Travis has supported me constantly (and I'm a lot of trouble!) over the last 15 years; I would not be the writer or the person I am today without her teaching, her mentorship, and, most important, our friendship (I hope I still live up to my motto). I also appreciate the kind words and advice that Amy Berkowitz, Sean H. Doyle, Sonya Huber, Leslie Jamison, Tao Lin, Joshua Mohr, and Haley Sherif offered me at various points in the writing and publication process. Amy Shearn, Heather Aimee O'Neill, and Emma Straub deserve special thanks, too, for recognizing and encouraging my ambitions.

I'm grateful to the editors who published earlier versions of these essays: Seth Abramson, Jessie Damiani, and Douglas Kearney of *Best American Experimental Writing 2015* ("Product Warning"); Dan Cafaro at *The Atticus Review* ("Denial"); the editors at *Crab Fat Magazine* ("Pharmacies of New York"); Jodee Stanley and the staff at *Ninth Letter* ("Use and Abuse"), Christopher Citro and Jason L. Jordan at *deCOMP* (the motel-key essays), Jason Teal, Chas Hoppe, and Ally Harris at *Heavy Feather Review* ("Relapse"); and Cheyenne L. Black and Edward Derbes at *Hayden's Ferry Review* ("A Glossary of Terms"). I'm also grateful to *Lit Hub* for republishing "Relapse" and Aaron Gilbreath at *Longreads* for finding and republishing "Use and Abuse." Thank you to Robert Atwan for naming "Use and Abuse" a Notable Essay in *Best American Essays 2018*.

My parents and sisters deserve extra-special recognition for their love and patience (sorry, guys). Same to anyone else who appears in the book (I can't name you here and also give you pseudonyms; you're the ones who wanted privacy!). Thanks, Lindsey Creel (you'll be in the next one), Starla Couso, the Bobal-Hansfords, Kim Kennedy, Mallory Szymanski, and Roxie Wilson. Dave and Chris, I appreciate your advice and support.

Maddie Rakic, I'm stoked to keep working together. Love to Emily Dufton and the rest of the *Points* family. Same to Ray. Todd, Dawn, and Victor, I've been so lucky to have you. Thank you.

RECENT CLEVELAND STATE UNIVERSITY POETRY CENTER PUBLICATIONS

ESSAYS

I Liked You Better Before I Knew You So Well by James Allen Hall

A Bestiary by Lily Hoang

The Leftovers by Shaelyn Smith

TRANSLATION

I Burned at the Feast: Selected Poems of Arseny Tarkovsky translated by Philip Metres and Dimitri Psurtsev

for a complete list of titles visit www.csupoetrycenter.com